Ouch!

how your body makes it through a very bad day

Written by
RICHARD WALKER

LONDON, NEW YORK, MUNICH,
PARIS, MELBOURNE, AND DELHI

PROJECT EDITOR
Andrea Mills
DESIGNER
Samantha Richiardi
SENIOR ART EDITOR
Joanne Little
MANAGING EDITOR
Linda Esposito
MANAGING ART EDITOR
Diane Thistlethwaite
DESIGN DEVELOPMENT MANAGER
Sophia M. Tampakopoulos Turner
PUBLISHING MANAGER
Andrew Macintyre
CATEGORY PUBLISHER
Laura Buller
PICTURE RESEARCHERS
Martin Copeland, Rob Nunn
PRODUCTION CONTROLLER
Michelle Ripton
DTP DESIGNER
Andy Hilliard
JACKET DESIGNERS
Akiko Kato
JACKET EDITOR
Mariza O'Keeffe
ILLUSTRATIONS
NIKID Design Ltd.
CONSULTANT
Dr. Sue Davidson

This edition published in the United States in 2009
by DK Publishing, Inc.
375 Hudson Street
New York, New York 10014

09 10 11 12 13 10 9 8 7 6 5 4 3 2 1

Copyright © 2009 Dorling Kindersley Limited

A catalog record for this book
is available from the Library of Congress.

ISBN: 978-0-7566-5813-7

Hi-res workflow proofed by
Colourscan, Singapore
Printed & bound by Hung Hing, China

Discover more at
www.dk.com

contents

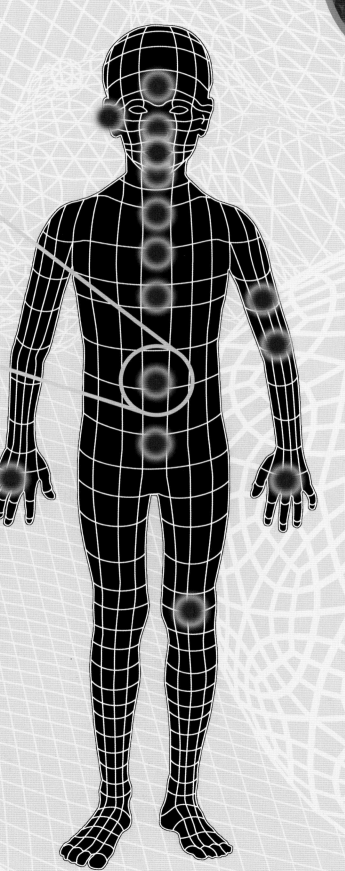

foreword

by Richard Walker

Right now there are thousands of things happening inside your body without you knowing anything about them. Did you know, for example, that as you read these words, your body's defense forces are busy battling marauding germs and bugs? Or are waiting on standby ready to tackle everyday hazards such as cuts, stings, burns, choking, or overheating? All to keep you alive and healthy.

It's too bad, then, that you can't see these and many other amazing events in action. Well, now you can!

Ouch! reveals a world previously unseen. Using brand new, computer-generated images and specially created 3-D animations, this groundbreaking book will show you what no other book can. For the first time you'll be able to view close-up—and often in gory detail—how your body deals daily with problems and emergencies.

During a jaw-dropping tour of the body you'll visit a whole host of locations. You'll be a front row spectator watching from all angles as evil invaders are repelled and destroyed or automatic defenses swing into action. Witness germ-filled droplets being blasted out of the nostrils, stand back as a pus-filled pimple explodes, and ride waves of urine gushing out of the bladder. Or, plunge into a churning stomach preparing to vomit, learn how ears repel bugs, and see the scab-making team in action.

With so much to explore in this hidden world of attack and defense, there's no time to waste. It's time to find out for yourself exactly what's going on inside you.

MEET NANOCAM

The incredibly small, hugely high-tech body explorer Nanocam is the shape of things to come.

As it prowls and patrols, Nanocam provides breaking news from the front lines of the body battlefield. Whether it is swimming in streams of hot, gushing blood, or filming the explosive action of a germ-packed sneeze, Nanocam travels everywhere to provide data readouts on this day of disasters. Bristling with cameras and amazing gadgets, no mission is too tough for Nanocam to tackle.

CAMERA CAPSULE
Nanocam is based on existing technology. A camera capsule is swallowed like a pill and passes through the intestines, filming them along the way.

REMOTE CAMERA
can access places that the main camera cannot reach.

MAIN CAMERA
includes the lens, automatic focus, and exposure, all protected by the clear dome.

LASER
can deploy its high-energy beam to gain access to difficult areas of the body.

NANOCAM'S EXTERIOR

Since its exterior is shiny, compact, and streamlined, Nanocam can glide effortlessly through any part of the body. Its smooth exterior resists damage by digestive enzymes and other bodily fluids and does not attract the unwanted attention of the hungry white blood cells that hunt down and eat any troublesome invaders.

SMOOTH COATING
protects and streamlines Nanocam so it can move easily around the body.

EMERGENCY INDICATOR
is blue in normal conditions, but flashes red if the body comes under attack.

SELF-CLEANING LENS
wipes away cells and debris so the camera has a clear view.

MICROFOIL CASING
has tiny holes that allow thrust from the propeller to push Nanocam forward.

GRAPPLING HOOK
anchors Nanocam when it risks being swept away by fast-moving liquids.

NANOCAM'S GADGETS

Although it is tiny, Nanocam is packed with gadgets.
From a waxy ear to a slimy stomach, Nanocam changes
its smooth appearance to suit the surroundings it
is investigating. Suddenly, claws, cameras, a laser,
and other devices pop out to meet the demands and
challenges of each situation. Anchored in place by
its grappling hook and ever-alert to the next danger,
Nanocam probes, scans, monitors, and records,
before sending reports back to the outside world.

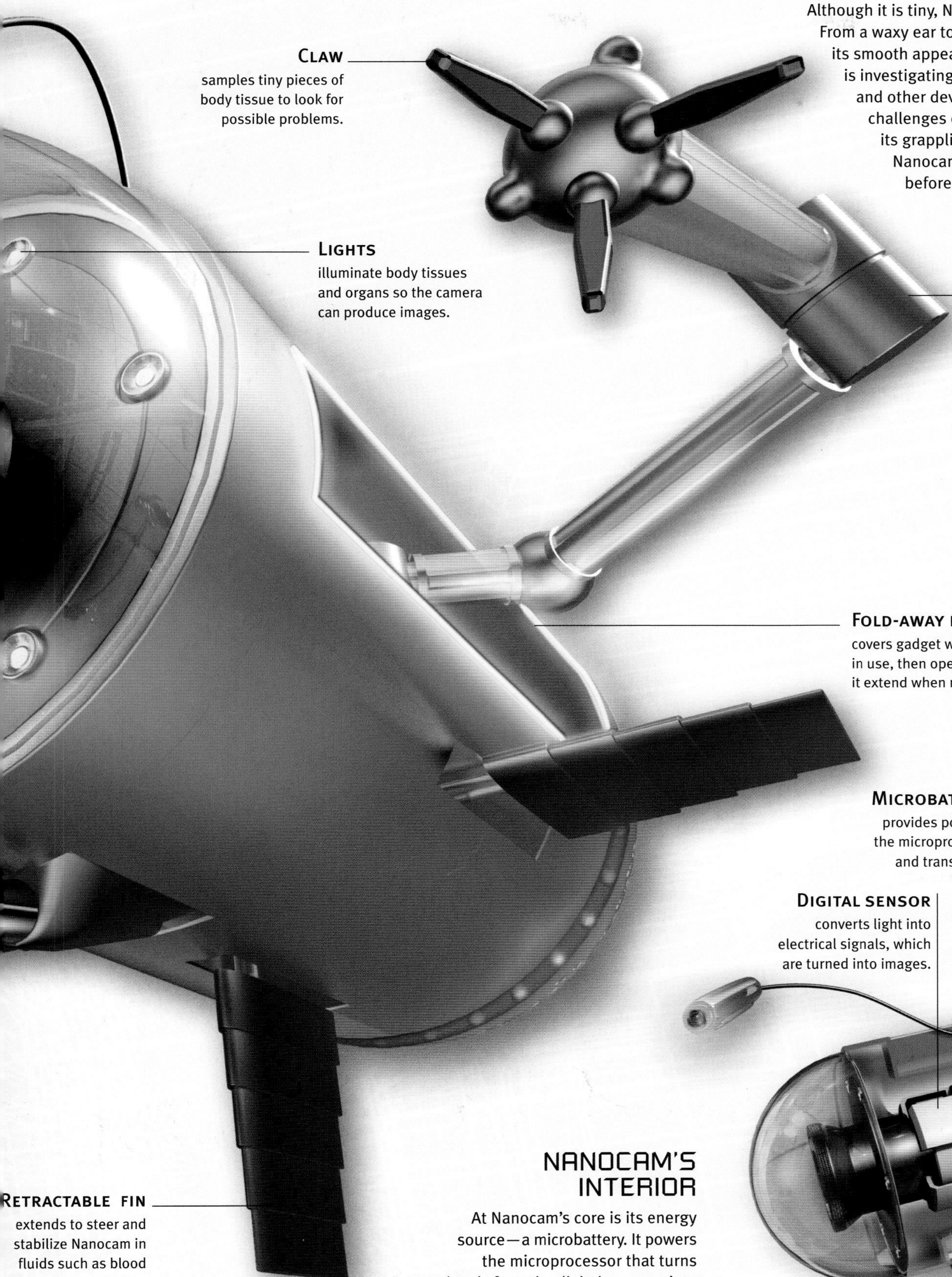

CLAW
samples tiny pieces of
body tissue to look for
possible problems.

LIGHTS
illuminate body tissues
and organs so the camera
can produce images.

RETRACTABLE ARM
allows gadget to extend
away from, or pull back
into, Nanocam.

FOLD-AWAY PANEL
covers gadget when not
in use, then opens to let
it extend when necessary.

MICROBATTERY
provides power to
the microprocessor
and transmitter.

PROPELLER
made of a lightweight
polymer, propels Nanocam
when it is on the move.

DIGITAL SENSOR
converts light into
electrical signals, which
are turned into images.

RETRACTABLE FIN
extends to steer and
stabilize Nanocam in
fluids such as blood
or urine.

NANOCAM'S INTERIOR

At Nanocam's core is its energy
source—a microbattery. It powers
the microprocessor that turns
signals from the digital cameras into
images and fires up the transmitter
that sends signals out of the body
so we can view Nanocam's pictures.
In addition, the microbattery powers
Nanocam's extendable gadgets, and
the motor that turns the propeller.

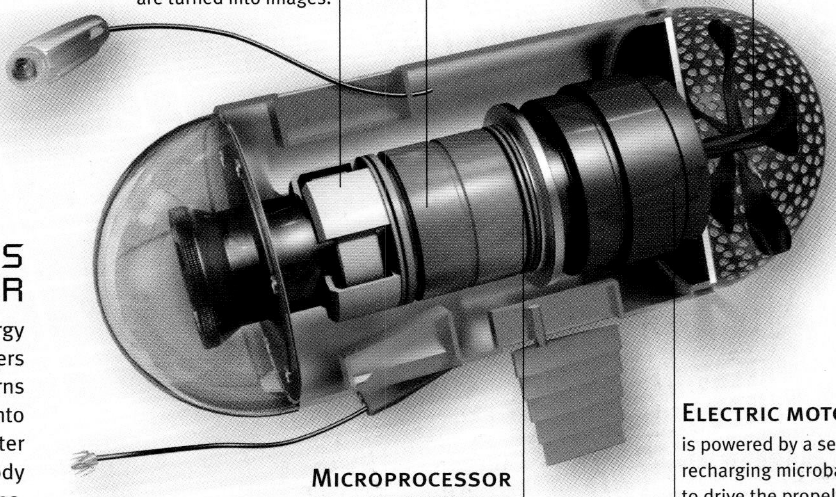

**MICROPROCESSOR
AND TRANSMITTER**
produces and stores images,
before transmitting them to a
computer outside the body.

ELECTRIC MOTOR
is powered by a self-
recharging microbattery
to drive the propeller.

Nasal cavity

Nostrils

Pollen grain

Pollen grain

Pollen grain

Bacteria

Dust particles

Rhinoviruses

Dust particles

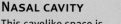

MUCUS
DROPLETS

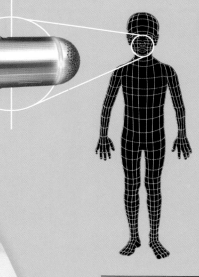

REFLEX EXPLOSION

With explosive force, a sneeze blasts up to 5,000 tiny droplets out of the nose and into the surrounding air at speeds of 95 mph (150 kph). Sneezing is a reflex action—automatic and unstoppable. It is triggered by itchy irritation inside the nose.

ENVIRONMENT:

Flung out of the nose by a sneeze, Nanocam captures the moment while hanging on with its grappling hook.

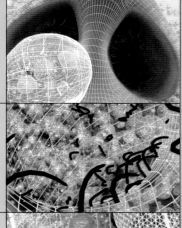

NASAL CAVITY

This cavelike space is just behind the nostrils. Its lining makes mucus and contains sensors that detect the irritants that cause sneezing.

MUCUS DROPLETS

These globules of watery mucus—the slimy, sticky, dirt-trapping fluid that coats the nasal cavity—remove viruses, pollen, and dust from the nose.

NOSTRILS

During normal breathing, nostrils carry air in and out of the nasal cavity. But during a sneeze, droplets explode from these two wide openings.

NOSE HAIRS

The force of the sneeze makes the nose hairs point outward. Normally, these hairs guard the nasal cavity, by trapping particles from breathed-in air.

RHINOVIRUSES

These rhinoviruses cause colds. They irritate the nasal lining and make it secrete extra mucus. Sneezing is a perfect way for viruses to infect others.

POLLEN GRAINS

Blown in the wind from grasses and other plants, pollen grains can inflame the nasal lining and cause a sneeze. A grain is 200 times bigger than a rhinovirus.

DUST PARTICLES

Cloth fibers and skin flakes form dust. A dust particle is thousands of times bigger than a rhinovirus. Big pieces are caught by nose hairs, but small ones irritate the nose.

NANOCAM REPORT: SNEEZING

Defense systems

When cells lining the nasal cavity and throat are infected by cold viruses, the immune (defense) system is activated. The body's responses initially cause cold symptoms such as a sore throat, a runny nose, and sneezing, but within a few days, defense chemicals and cells have wiped out the invading viruses.

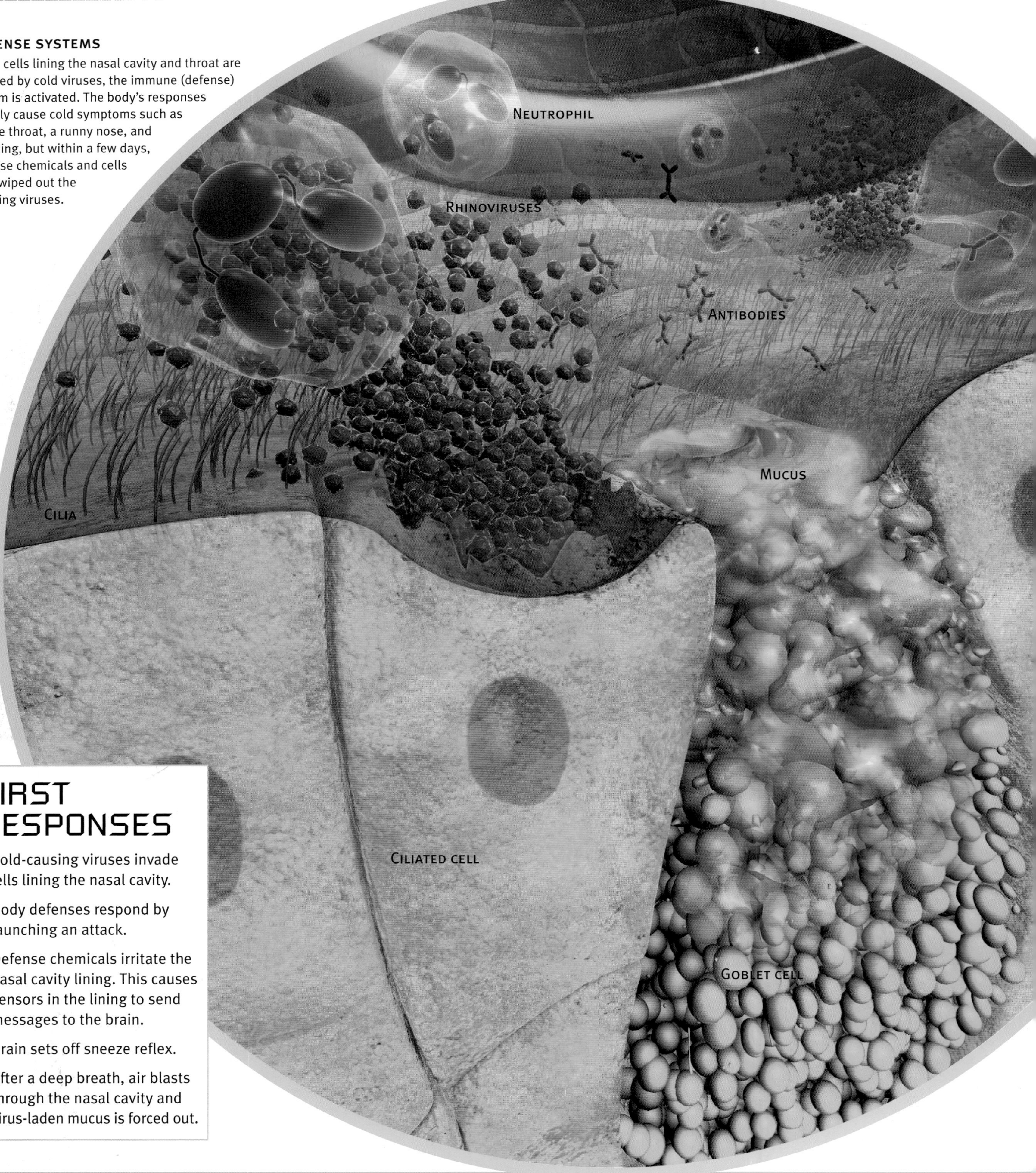

Neutrophil
Rhinoviruses
Antibodies
Mucus
Cilia
Ciliated cell
Goblet cell

FIRST RESPONSES

- Cold-causing viruses invade cells lining the nasal cavity.
- Body defenses respond by launching an attack.
- Defense chemicals irritate the nasal cavity lining. This causes sensors in the lining to send messages to the brain.
- Brain sets off sneeze reflex.
- After a deep breath, air blasts through the nasal cavity and virus-laden mucus is forced out.

DATA SEARCH

- The common cold can be caused by any one of more than 200 viruses.

- Most colds occur in fall and winter, probably because cold weather makes people spend more time together indoors, and this increases the chances of spreading cold viruses.

- Between January 1981 and September 1983, record-breaking British schoolgirl Donna Griffiths sneezed at least once every five minutes for 978 days. In the first year, Donna sneezed more than a million times.

- It is not just an itchy nose that causes sneezing. About 20 percent of people sneeze when suddenly exposed to bright light. This problem, called photic sneezing, is inherited from parents.

- Some people believe that if you sneeze with your eyes open, your eyeballs will pop out. But it is a complete myth. It is virtually impossible to open your eyelids when you sneeze—they snap shut automatically.

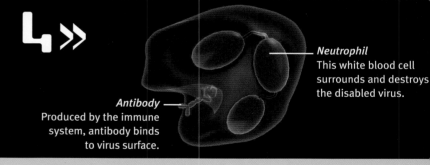

1 »

Virus
Minute parasite lands on a ciliated cell and enters.

Cilia
Hairlike structures covering surface of ciliated cell.

2 »

Rhinoviruses
Hundreds or thousands of rhinoviruses explode out of ciliated cell.

VIRUS OUTBREAK

Droplets carrying cold-causing rhinoviruses are breathed in to the nasal cavity. The cavity is lined with ciliated cells (a type of cell with cilia on the surface), which are targeted and entered by rhinoviruses. Viruses must invade cells to reproduce. Once inside, a virus takes over the cell's chemical mechanism to make many copies of itself.

EXPLOSION OF NEW VIRUSES

The infected ciliated cell bursts open to release lots of newly made viruses. Some invade neighboring ciliated cells in order to reproduce and make even more viruses. Others are sneezed out into the air, and breathed in by other people. Damaged and infected cells release chemicals that trigger the body's defenses.

3 »

Mucus
Thick, slimy fluid that causes nose blockage.

Goblet cell
Goblet-shaped, mucus-making cells step up production when infected by cold viruses.

4 »

Neutrophil
This white blood cell surrounds and destroys the disabled virus.

Antibody
Produced by the immune system, antibody binds to virus surface.

MUCUS SURGE

Cold symptoms are not produced by viruses but by defense chemicals released to fight infection. They cause goblet cells to secrete surplus mucus, resulting in a blocked nose and increased blood flow, which brings in extra white blood cells and causes inflammation. This triggers pain receptors, resulting in irritation and sneezing.

ANTIBODIES ON THE RAMPAGE

In the final phase of the battle, antibodies in the mucus layer target viruses and bind to them. The viruses can no longer invade any more cells. White blood cells—neutrophils and macrophages—mop up the disabled viruses and cell debris. The mucus now appears thick and green because of the huge number of white blood cells.

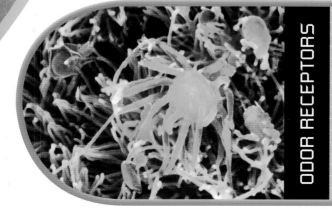

ODOR RECEPTORS

In addition to playing a part in breathing and sneezing, your nose detects odors. This highly magnified image (x 8,570) shows one of the millions of odor receptors (blue) in the upper part of the nasal cavity. It consists of a central bulb from which radiate hairlike cilia. The cilia respond to breathed-in scent molecules by sending messages to the brain so that you can smell odors. Your sense of smell goes when you have a cold because thick mucus stops scent molecules from reaching odor receptors.

7:15 A.M.—BATHROOM BREAK

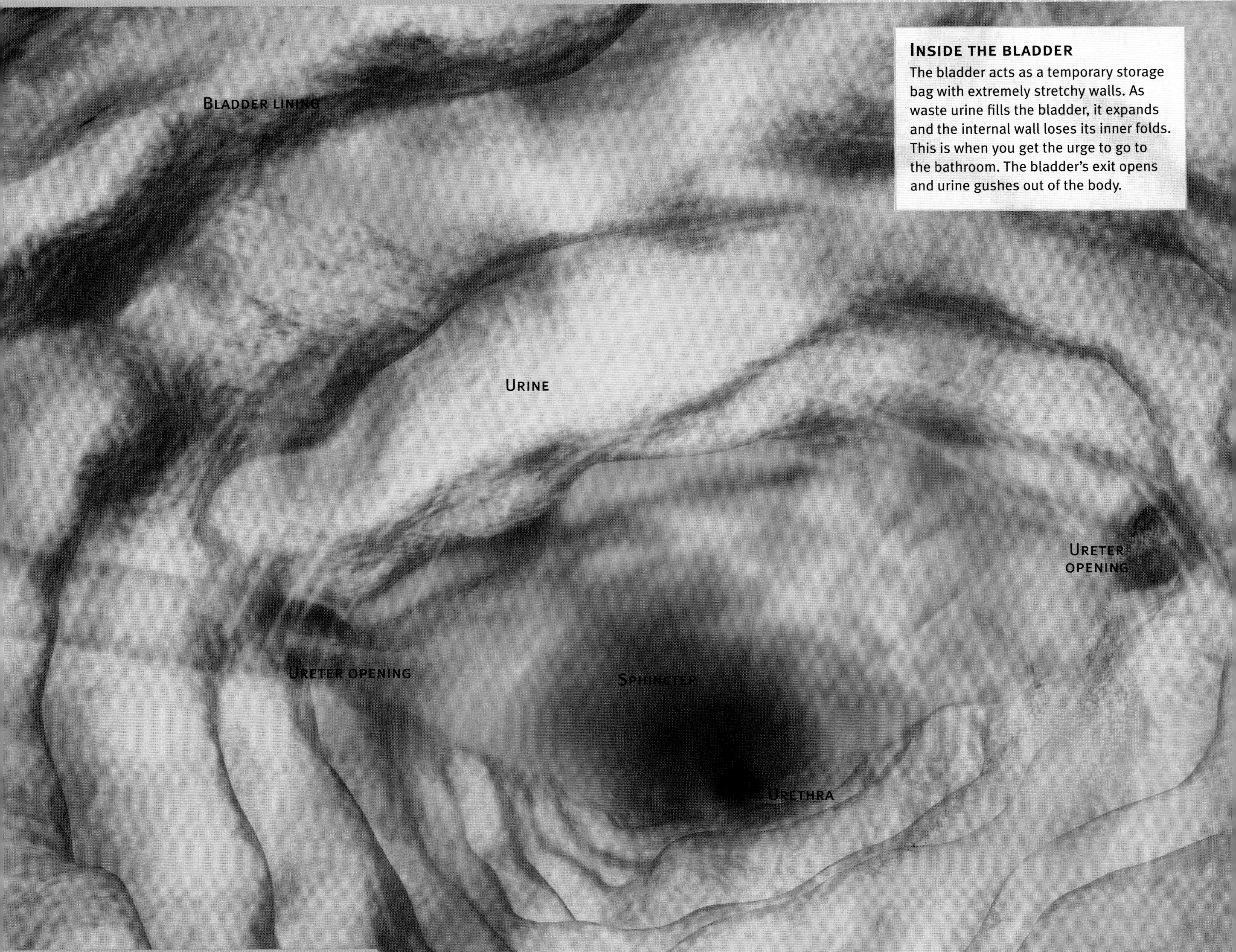

Bladder lining
Urine
Ureter opening
Ureter opening
Sphincter
Urethra

Inside the bladder

The bladder acts as a temporary storage bag with extremely stretchy walls. As waste urine fills the bladder, it expands and the internal wall loses its inner folds. This is when you get the urge to go to the bathroom. The bladder's exit opens and urine gushes out of the body.

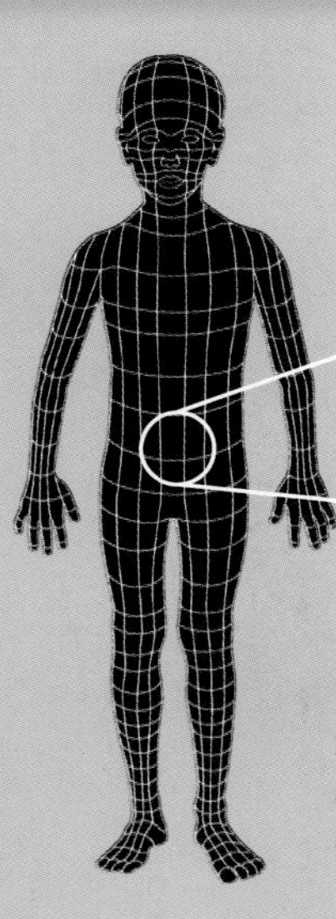

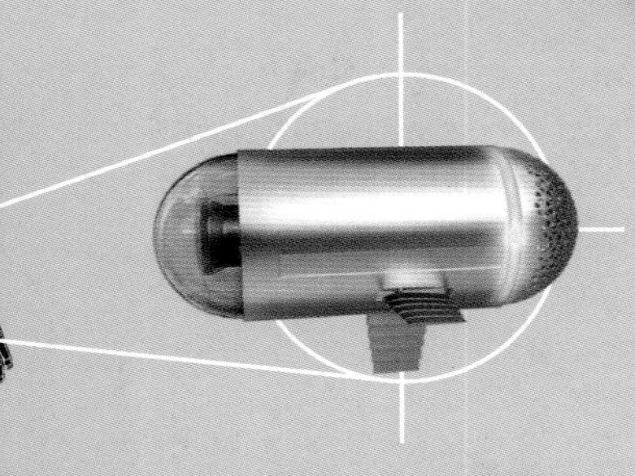

Environment:

Submerged in urine, Nanocam uses its fins and propeller to keep position while viewing a swirl of liquid escaping from the bladder.

WASTE DISPOSAL

Every day, each of us has to urinate, or pee. This is because body cells are constantly dumping waste into the bloodstream. If waste were left to build up, it would soon poison us. The body's two kidneys filter out the blood's waste and excess water to make urine. This gets stored in the bladder until it is released outside. Without a bladder, urine would trickle out continually.

FIRST RESPONSES

- As the bladder fills up with urine, its elastic, muscular wall stretches.

- Sensors in the bladder wall detect the stretching and send nerve messages to the brain.

- The need to urinate is recognized, so it is time for a bathroom break.

1 »

Ureter opening
This closes while the bladder is emptying to stop urine from flowing backward

2 »

Urine
The substance consists of 95 percent water and five percent dissolved wastes.

ARRIVING BY TUBE

Every few seconds urine is produced by the kidneys and transferred to the bladder by two tubes called ureters. Each ureter has an opening in the lower back part of the bladder. Muscles in the walls of the ureters contract rhythmically to push the urine down and into its temporary store, the bladder.

BLADDER AT BURSTING POINT

The space inside an empty bladder is about the size of a plum. But as urine continually seeps in, the interior stretches to the size of a grapefruit. Urine is yellow in color because it contains pigment (coloring) that is released into the blood when worn-out red blood cells are broken down by the body's liver.

3 »

Sphincter
The guard of the bladder exit opens to let urine escape.

4 »

Bladder lining
Folds reappear here as the bladder shrinks.

OPEN AND OUT

At the bottom of the bladder is the opening to the urethra, the tube that carries urine out of the body. This opening is surrounded by a ring of muscle called a sphincter, which is normally tightly shut. But during a bathroom break, the sphincter relaxes—under instructions from the brain—in preparation for the release of urine.

CONTINUOUS PROCESS

Given a signal from the brain, muscles in the bladder wall contract. This makes the bladder smaller, at the same time forcing urine out through the open exit into the urethra. Contractions continue until the urine has been expelled, the sphincter closes, and the bladder starts to refill once again.

DATA SEARCH

- In an average lifetime a person releases around 10,500 gallons (40,000 liters) of urine—enough to fill 270 bathtubs.

- Inside each kidney are about one million urine-making units called nephrons. These process 460 gallons (1,750 liters) of blood daily to make just 3 pints (1.5 liters) of urine.

- Sometimes the waste in urine forms crystals that grow inside the bladder to form "stones." Bladder stones may be painful and make it difficult to urinate, but they can be treated.

- Doctors used to diagnose disease by examining the color, smell, and even taste of urine. Today, doctors use chemical tests to analyze urine.

- Since babies cannot control their bladder sphincters, diapers can collect the leakages.

BONE PROTECTION

Shaping and supporting our body is a flexible skeleton made of a bony framework that allows us to move while protecting our tissues and organs.

Bones are living organs made of a unique combination of calcium salts and flexible collagen. This mix makes them hard but not brittle, and able to take the stresses of everyday knocks and jolts. Each bone consists of outer dense tissue with a strong, lightweight interior. Bones contain tissue that make blood cells. These carry oxygen and fight infection. The skeleton protects soft organs such as the brain, spinal cord, and bladder from harm.

COMPACT BONE

This cross-section shows the structure of compact, or cortical, bone—the dense outer layer of bone. It is made from microscopic cylinders called osteons. Running in parallel rows along the bone, osteons act as weight-bearing pillars to give compact bone its immense strength. In the middle of each osteon is a central canal that carries blood vessels and nerves.

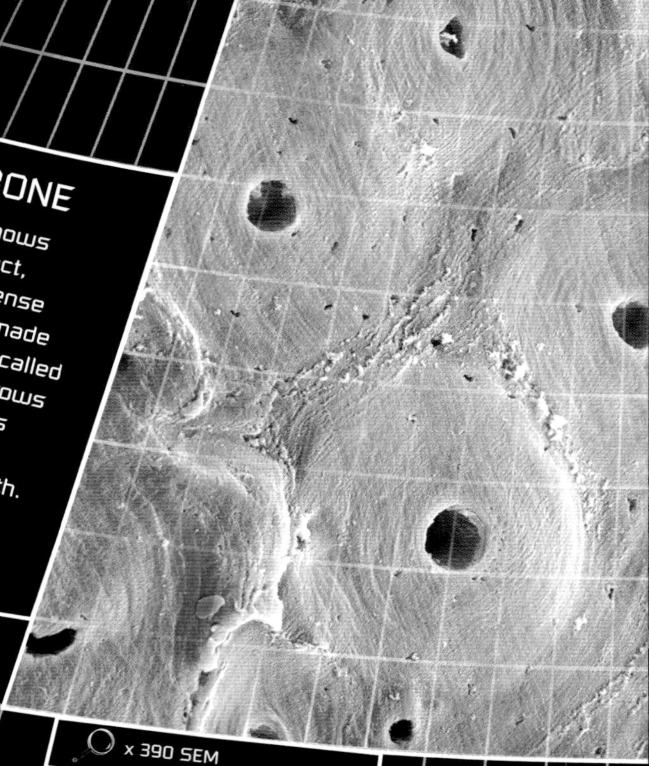

x 390 SEM

LINKED BY AROUND 400 JOINTS, THERE ARE 206 BONES IN A HUMAN SKELETON, WHICH MAKES UP 20 PERCENT OF BODY WEIGHT.

x 45 SEM

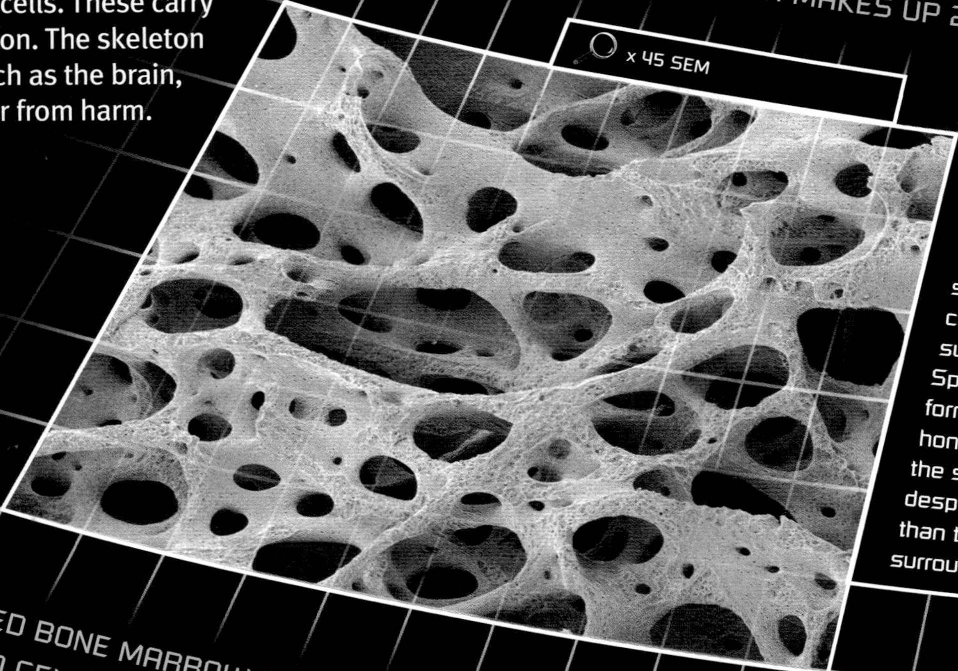

SPONGY BONE

Although it is called spongy, this type of bone tissue is neither soft nor squishy. Instead, it is constructed from a network of rigid supports with spaces in between. Spongy, or cancellous, bone tissue forms the inner part of bones. The honeycomblike structure provides the strength to resist daily stresses, despite being much lighter in weight than the dense compact bone that surrounds it.

EACH SECOND, RED BONE MARROW PRODUCES TWO MILLION RED BLOOD CELLS WHILE THE SPLEEN AND LIVER REMOVE TWO MILLION OLD CELLS FROM THE BLOOD.

RED BONE MARROW

This soft tissue (orange) is found in the spaces within spongy bone (blue). Its vital role is to manufacture all three types of blood cells—red and white blood cells and platelets. Blood cells that are worn out must be replaced. In young children red marrow is found in all bones, but in adults only certain bones, such as the shoulder blades and skull, contain it.

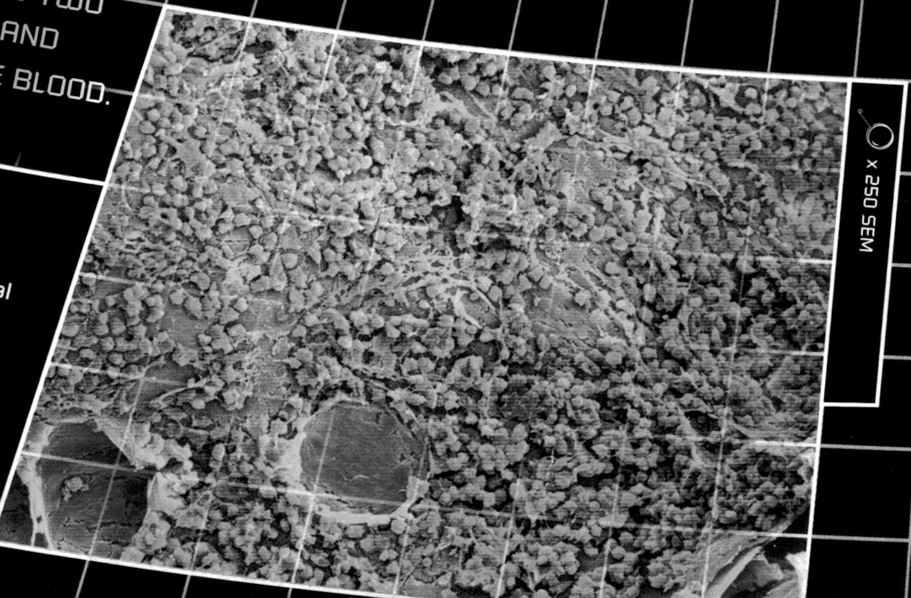

x 250 SEM

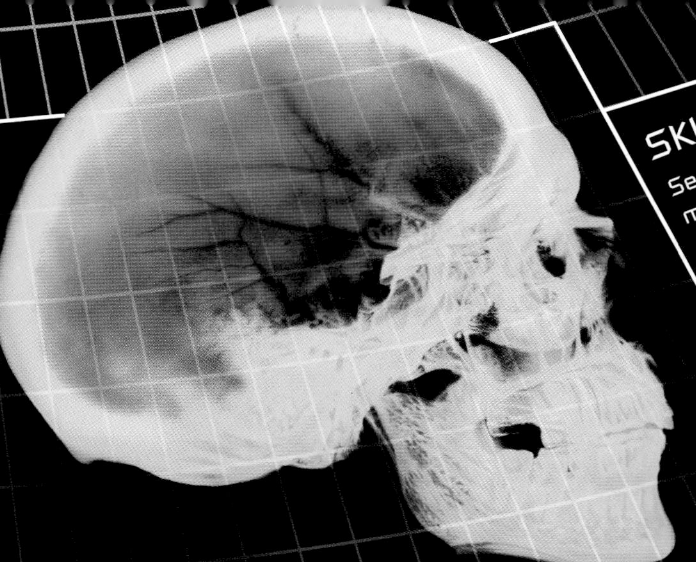

SKULL BONES

Seen here in side view, the skull is made of 22 bones. Most of the bones are held together by sutures, rigid joints that give the structure great strength. Eight cranial bones form a domed casing called the cranium. This surrounds and protects the brain. Fourteen facial bones underpin the face, hold the eyeballs in secure sockets, house the organs of smell and taste, and provide anchorage for the teeth. Only the mandible (lower jaw) moves, allowing us to eat and speak.

x 0.4 Colored X-ray

SPINE

Extending from head to hips, the spine (or backbone) forms the body's central axis, supporting and balancing the skull and upper body. It also forms a protective "tunnel" around the spinal cord, which extends down the back from the brain. The spine is a chain of 26 bones called vertebrae, between which are shock-absorbing cartilage disks that give it flexibility. Shown here from a back view are the five big lumbar vertebrae that carry most of the body's weight.

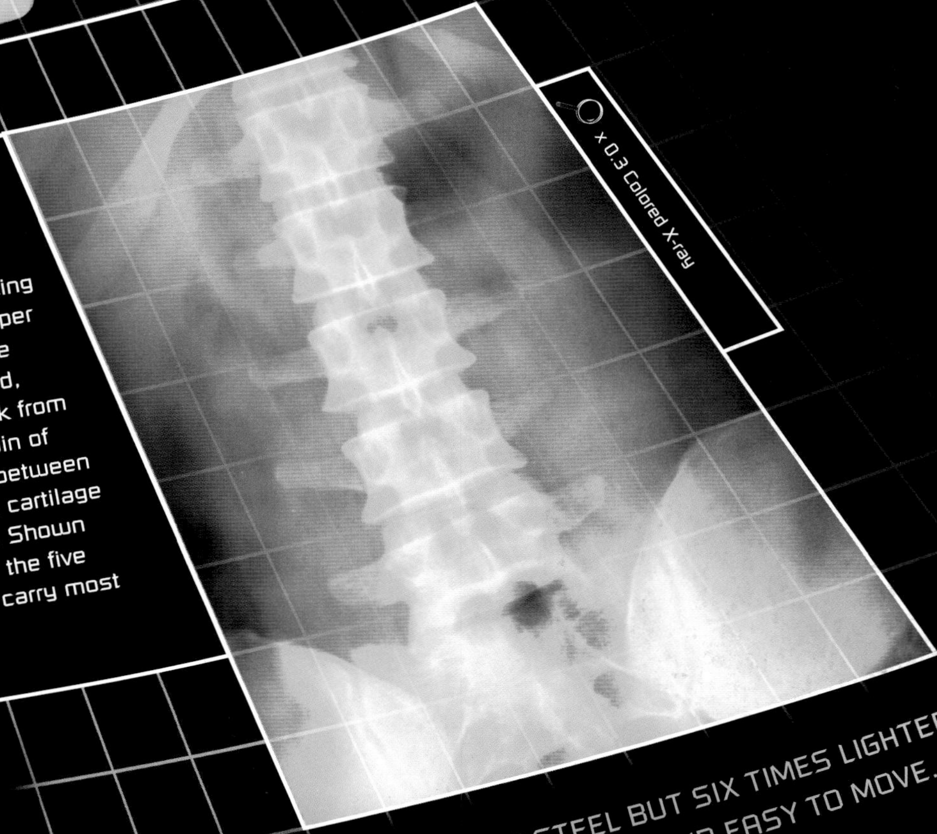

x 0.3 Colored X-ray

COUGHING OR LAUGHING PUTS MUCH MORE STRAIN ON THE BACKBONE THAN WALKING OR STANDING.

BONES ARE CONSTANTLY RESHAPING THEMSELVES—THE EQUIVALENT OF THE ENTIRE SKELETON IS REPLACED EVERY SEVEN YEARS.

BONE IS AS STRONG AS STEEL BUT SIX TIMES LIGHTER, MAKING THE SKELETON ROBUST AND EASY TO MOVE.

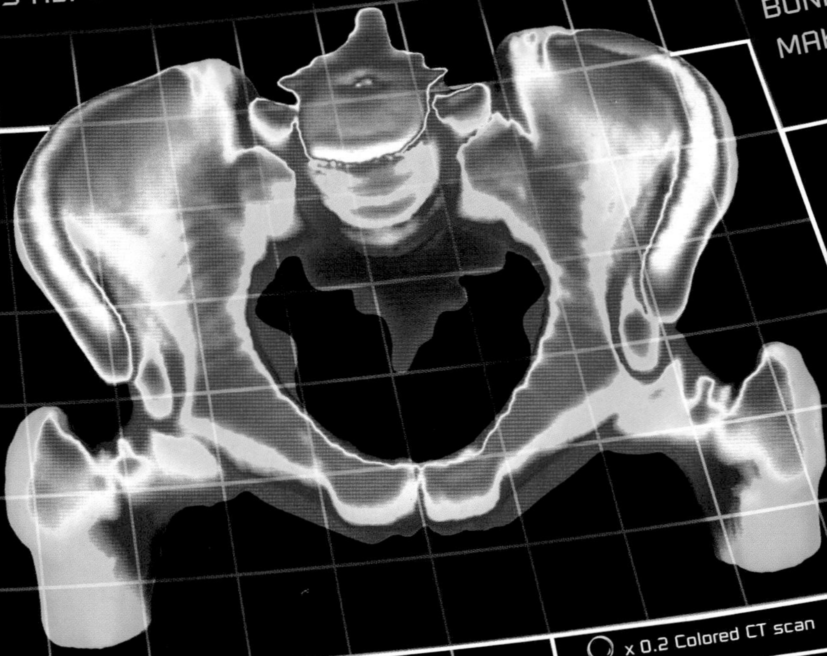

PELVIC BONES

This scan shows the basin-shaped pelvis and the tops of the thighbones (lower left and right) that are attached to it. The pelvis consists of the pelvic girdle and the sacrum, part of the backbone. The pelvic girdle has two curved pelvic bones that join at the front and are firmly attached to the sacrum at the back. The pelvis supports and protects the digestive, urinary, and reproductive organs, as well as attaching the legs to the body and anchoring the muscles that move the leg.

x 0.2 Colored CT scan

SKIN
BACTERIA

FINGERTIP

INFLAMMATION

FINGERNAIL

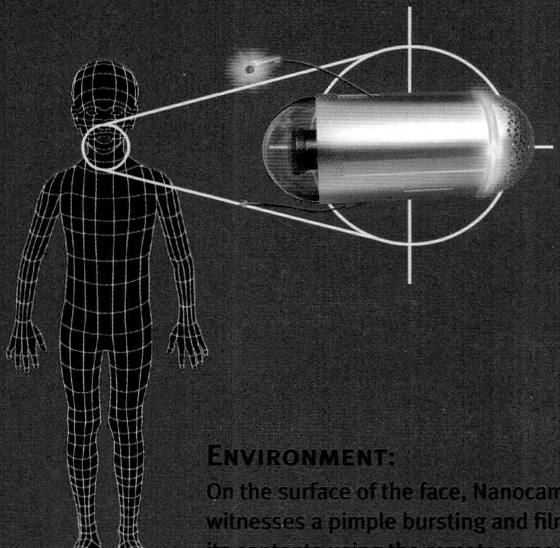

BURSTING OUT

Although people are warned not to squeeze pimples, some cannot resist it. Here, two fingertips apply pressure on each side of an inflamed and bulging pimple. Like a volcanic eruption, the top of the pimple opens up and a spurt of whitish fluid laden with bacteria bursts out of the skin and into the air.

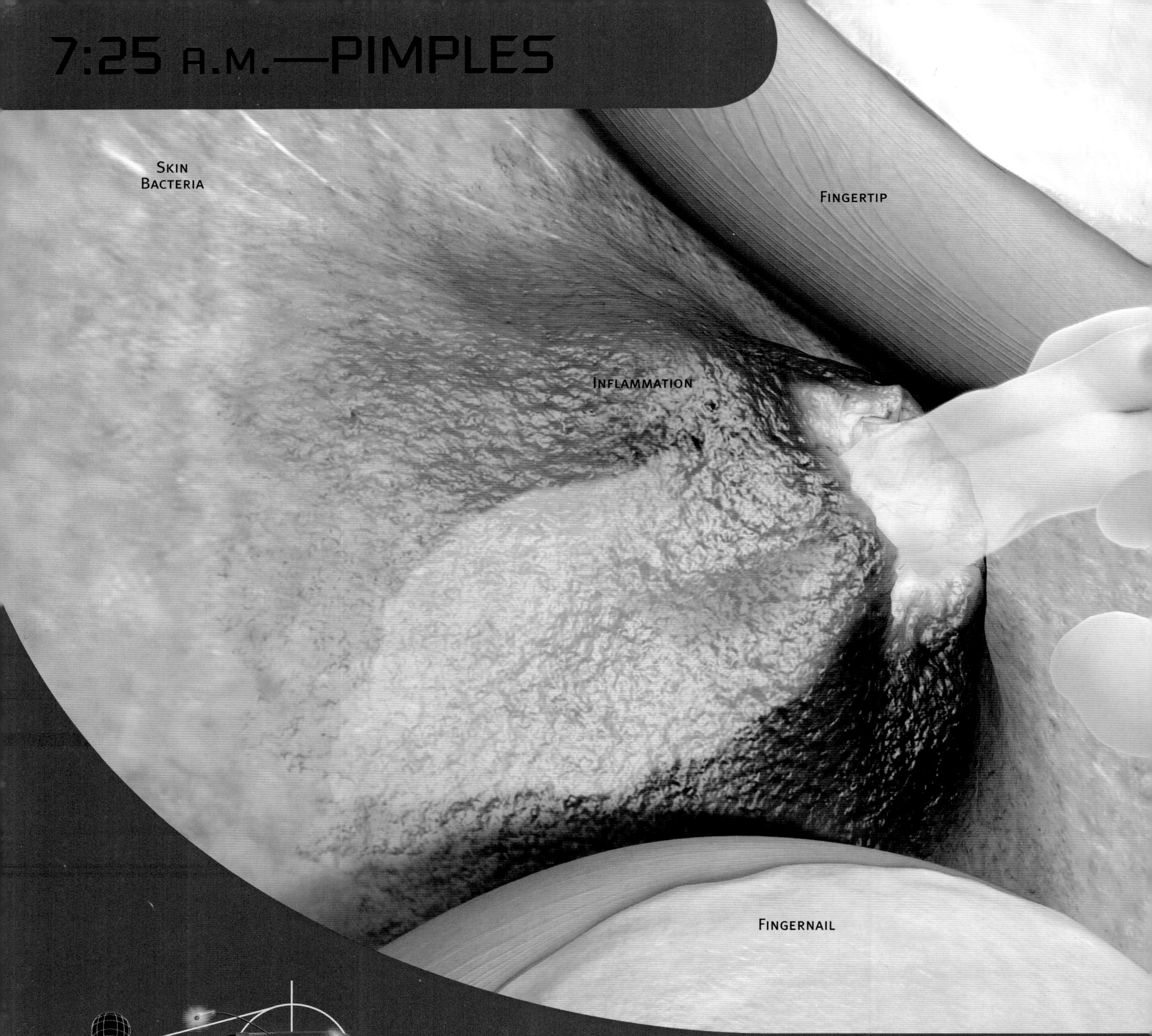

ENVIRONMENT:
On the surface of the face, Nanocam witnesses a pimple bursting and films its contents using the remote camera.

SPLIT EPIDERMIS
The forced action of pushing out the contents of the pimple splits open a small section of the epidermis—the tough, upper layer of the skin.

PIMPLE BACTERIA
Various types of bacteria, including the *Staphylococcus* shown here, multiply in the blockage under the skin. This forms a pimple, causing infection.

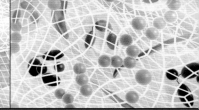

PUS

NEUTROPHIL

SKIN CELL

STAPHYLOCOCCUS
BACTERIUM

DEAD NEUTROPHIL
AND BACTERIA

DEAD SKIN CELLS
Flattened, dead skin cells are continually lost from the surface of the epidermis. When a pimple is picked, these cells get mixed up with the contents.

WHITE BLOOD CELLS
A key part of the immune (defense) system, neutrophils (white blood cells) flood into the pimple area to surround, eat, and destroy the bacteria.

PUS
This thick, whitish-yellow fluid contains a build-up of dead skin cells, debris, oily sebum, and living and dead white blood cells engorged with bacteria.

INFLAMED TISSUE
One of the body's responses to infection is inflammation. Red, sore tissue around the pimple is the result of extra blood rushing to defend the site.

BEWARE...
Do not squeeze pimples, especially if they look red and inflamed. Squeezing can force the pimple's contents deeper into the skin. Not only does pimple-picking enable the skin's existing bacteria to enter the wound and possibly cause an infection, but the burst pimple can also leave a permanent scar on the skin.

NANOCAM REPORT: PIMPLES

FIRST RESPONSES

- Bacteria invade a blocked hair follicle (pit in the skin from which a hair grows) and their waste products activate the body's defenses.
- Pain sensors in inflamed pimple send messages to brain; soreness is recognized.
- Visual recognition of raised, red blemish with whitish core.
- Washing skin with soap helps to loosen the blockage.

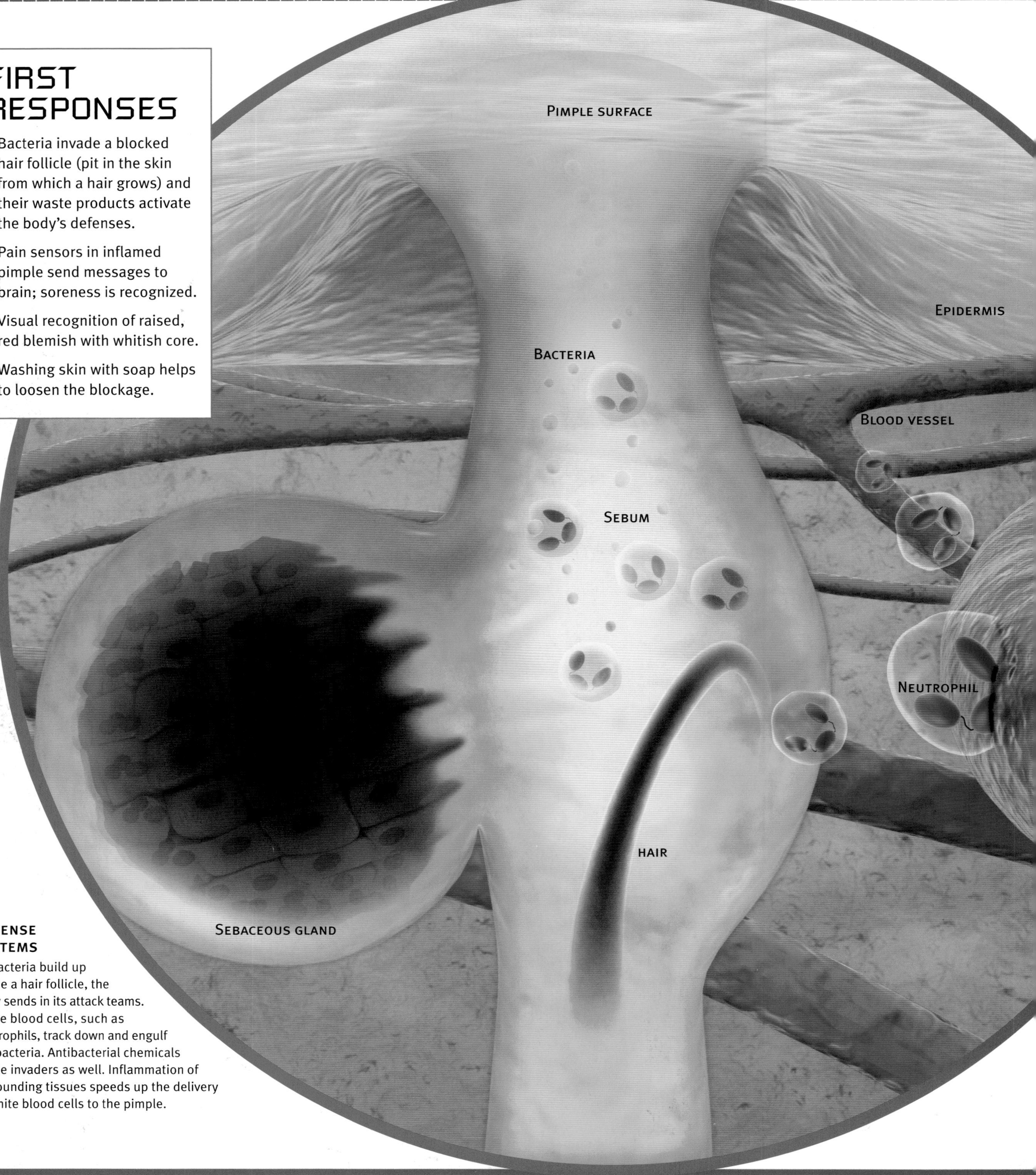

Pimple surface
Epidermis
Bacteria
Blood vessel
Sebum
Neutrophil
Hair
Sebaceous gland

Defense systems

As bacteria build up inside a hair follicle, the body sends in its attack teams. White blood cells, such as neutrophils, track down and engulf the bacteria. Antibacterial chemicals tackle invaders as well. Inflammation of surrounding tissues speeds up the delivery of white blood cells to the pimple.

DATA SEARCH

- Pimples affect young people mainly, peaking in number during the teenage years. This is because changing hormone levels in puberty can make the skin more oily. A severe outbreak of pimples, characterized by multiple infected pimples and possible scarring, is called acne.

- It is a myth that eating chocolate or fried foods causes pimples. However, a good diet that includes fresh fruit and vegetables and drinking plenty of water helps skin to be healthy.

- Unfortunately, pimples cannot be washed away. In fact, too much washing can dry out the skin. The body then reacts by producing even more oily sebum than normal, making spots more likely. Washing twice a day with a mild soap is the best recommendation.

- Air pollution can increase pimple production by blocking pores in the skin. Changing hormone levels during a girl's periods—or during times of general stress—may make skin more oily and prone to pimples.

 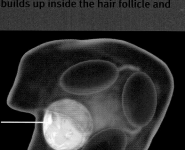

Sebaceous gland
Produces sebum—an oily fluid that normally keeps skin moisturized and supple.

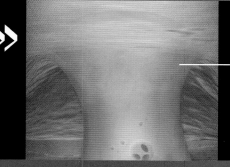

Bacteria
Multiply by dividing into two new bacterial cells.

TRAPPED SEBUM

Young people experience an increase in the production of the oily substance sebum. When sebum is released from a sebaceous gland, it enters a hair follicle and narrows the opening. Unable to escape onto the skin's surface, sebum builds up inside the hair follicle and sebaceous gland.

RISE AND RISE OF BACTERIA

Although bacteria normally live harmlessly on the skin's surface, they are attracted to nutritious sebum, leading them to invade the swollen hair follicle. Bacteria become sealed inside the growing pimple by a cap of sebum and dead skin cells that plugs the upper part of the hair follicle. As they feed, bacteria divide and increase in number rapidly.

Neutrophil
A white blood cell that engulfs and eats bacteria.

Inflammation
Caused by increased blood flow to the infected pimple.

NEUTROPHILS LEAD THE HUNT

The presence of bacteria in the hair follicle sends out signals that are detected by neutrophils carried in the bloodstream. These white blood cell hunters exit blood capillaries to enter the infected hair follicle where they locate, surround, and digest the bacteria. Engorged with bacteria, neutrophils die, mixing with sebum, debris, and bacteria to form pus.

INFLAMED FOLLICLE

Chemicals released by bacteria and cells in the hair follicle combine to trigger inflammation. Blood vessels surrounding the hair follicle become wider and leakier. As well as allowing neutrophils to enter, fluid carrying bacteria-killing chemicals can seep into the follicle. Together with pus, this makes the pimple red, swollen, and sore.

BLACKHEAD

A blackhead is a type of pimple in which the hair follicle is capped by a plug of dark material. This magnified image (x 150) shows such a plug surrounding a hair that has been pulled out of the follicle. The dark color of the blackhead cap is not caused by dirt. Instead it contains melanin, the pigment that colors skin and which turns black on exposure to oxygen in the air. The melanin comes from dead skin cells that form part of the plug.

8:00 A.M.—BRUSHING TEETH

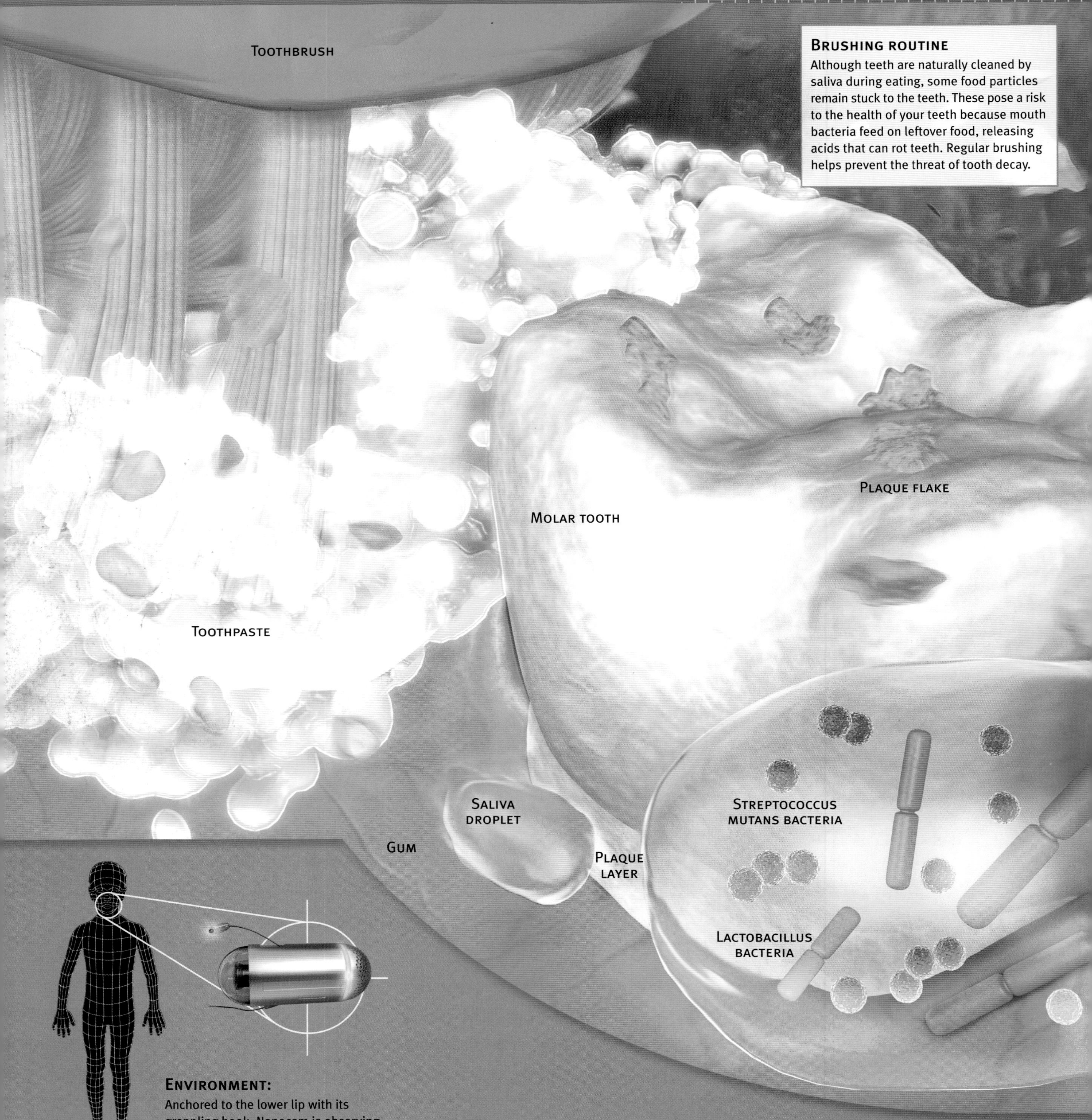

Toothbrush
Toothpaste
Molar tooth
Plaque flake
Saliva droplet
Gum
Plaque layer
Streptococcus mutans bacteria
Lactobacillus bacteria

Brushing routine

Although teeth are naturally cleaned by saliva during eating, some food particles remain stuck to the teeth. These pose a risk to the health of your teeth because mouth bacteria feed on leftover food, releasing acids that can rot teeth. Regular brushing helps prevent the threat of tooth decay.

Environment:

Anchored to the lower lip with its grappling hook, Nanocam is observing a toothbrush at work inside the mouth.

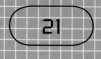
DOWN IN THE MOUTH

Your teeth play a key role in digestion. From the chisel-shaped ones at the front to the big, broad ones at the back, teeth cut and crush saliva-drenched food into small pieces ready for swallowing. Your mouth is also home to a permanent population of bacteria. Most are beneficial, stopping harmful bacteria form moving in, but some can cause tooth decay and gum disease.

FIRST RESPONSES

- Tongue detects a "furry" feel to the teeth and a stale taste in the mouth.
- Brain decides it is time to brush teeth and freshen breath.
- Toothbrush is loaded with toothpaste and teeth are cleaned using a circular motion and short back and forth movements.

1 »

Cusps
These raised edges crush food when teeth in upper and lower jaws bite together.

2 »

Plaque
Film that covers surface and crevices of tooth and junction with gums.

SEALED AND SECURE

Located near the back of the mouth, this molar tooth, like all the other teeth, is anchored in a socket in the jaw by its roots. Pink gums cover the jawbone and seal shut the entrance to the socket. Above the gum projects the crown of the tooth, which is covered by rock-hard white enamel.

PROBLEM PLAQUE

These teeth were not brushed last night, so by morning plaque has built up. Plaque is a whitish-yellow film made up of microscopic fibers, old food, and bacteria that sticks firmly to teeth. If plaque is allowed to accumulate, bacteria will thrive by feeding on food remains and releasing acids that eat away at the protective tooth enamel.

3 »

Toothbrush bristles
Used to brush the top, sides, and base of each tooth.

4 »

Droplet
Contains several types of mouth bacteria that can cause tooth decay.

BRISTLES FIGHT BACK

A toothbrush is used in the battle against plaque. Tough, fine bristles scrape plaque from the teeth, assisted by foamy, abrasive toothpaste. Bristles are moved up and down, and around and around, to clear plaque out from every nook and cranny of the teeth. Gentle brushing of the gums clears plaque from the base of the teeth.

BACTERIA GIVEN THE BRUSH OFF

Droplets of saliva and diluted toothpaste are splashed out as the toothbrush removes the traces of plaque. These droplets contain plaque bacteria such as *Streptococcus mutans*, a normal inhabitant of the mouth, which can cause damage such as tooth decay and gum disease. Regular flossing with dental floss also helps keep gums healthy.

DATA SEARCH

- The hardest substance in the body is tooth enamel. Unfortunately, enamel does not contain any living cells to repair itself if damaged, so dentists must fill the cavities.
- Regularly consuming sugary food and drinks increases the risk of tooth decay. Bacteria feast on sugars to release acids.
- People have two sets of teeth in a lifetime. The first set of 20 baby teeth is replaced by 32 permanent teeth during childhood.

- The earliest toothbrushes date back thousands of years. A "chew stick" was made by chewing one end of a twig to make a crude brush.
- Salt, dried flowers, lizard liver, and human urine were all ancient versions of toothpaste.

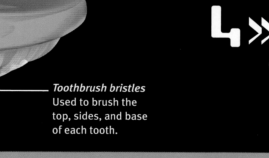

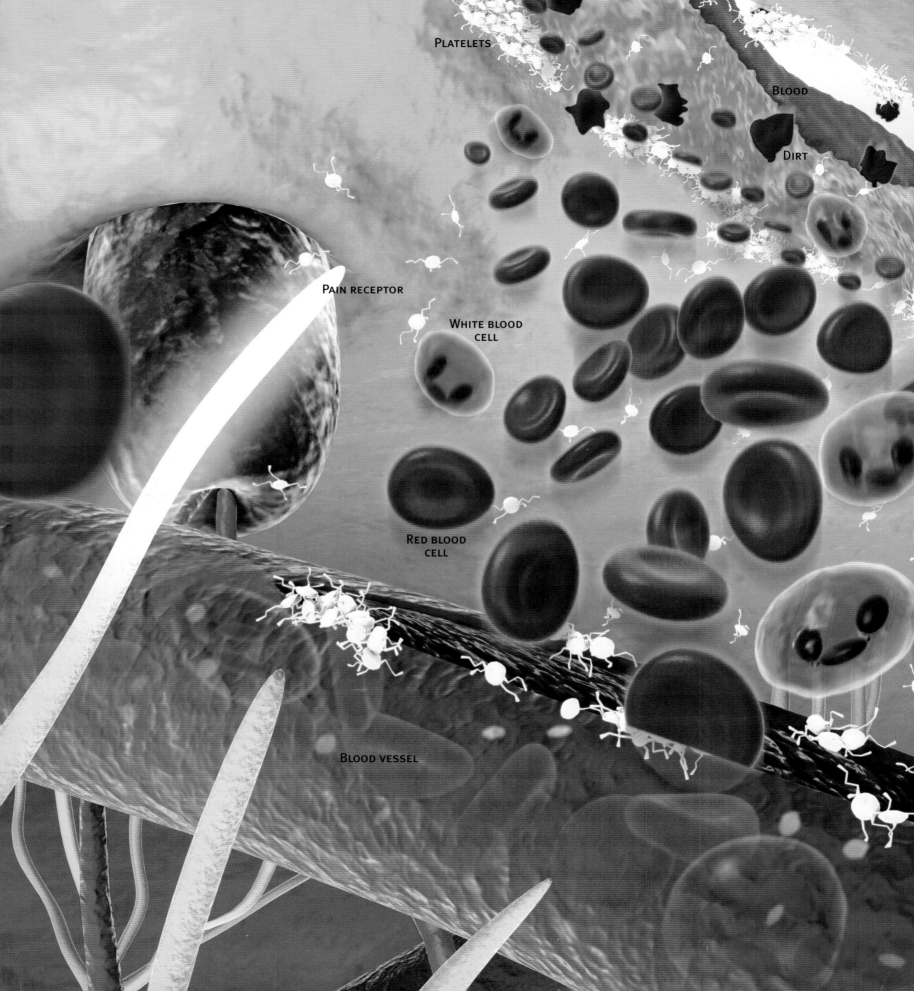

Broken skin

Platelets

Blood

Dirt

Pain receptor

White blood cell

Red blood cell

Blood vessel

LOSING BLOOD

A fall on a gritty road has cut skin on the knee. Immediately, blood begins to trickle from the painful wound because blood vessels just under the skin have been broken. A defense mechanism—called hemostasis—swings into action to stop bleeding by reducing the blood flow and plugging the leak.

ENVIRONMENT:

Nanocam is under a cut in the skin monitoring a leaking blood vessel.

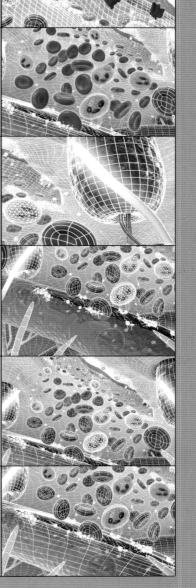

BROKEN SKIN

The skin, which normally provides a protective barrier, is scraped and cut open so that delicate tissues are exposed to the outside world.

DIRT AND GRIT

On contact with the road, particles of dirt and grit are forced into the cut in the skin. These cause irritation and may introduce germs to the wound.

LEAKING BLOOD

Deeper in the skin, the fall has sliced open a blood vessel. The blood carried by the vessel leaks through the surrounding tissues to the outside.

PAIN RECEPTOR

The torn tissues, together with chemicals released from the damaged cells, stimulate the pain receptors. These fire off signals to the brain, and pain is felt.

BLOOD VESSEL

The combination of damage to the blood vessel and reaction to pain triggers vascular spasm—the leaky vessel gets narrower, greatly reducing blood loss.

PLATELETS

These tiny disk-shaped cells in the blood are activated at the wound site. They stick to each other, forming a plug to limit the bleeding.

WHITE BLOOD CELLS

Macrophages and neutrophils are both types of white blood cell. They pass into the damaged tissue, looking for invading bacteria to destroy.

DEFENSE SYSTEMS

Without the body's automatic clotting system, the smallest of cuts could cause catastrophic blood loss. Just 20 seconds after an injury to a blood vessel, whether in the skin or deeper in the body, cell fragments in the blood called platelets trigger the process that forms a clot to seal the leaking wound.

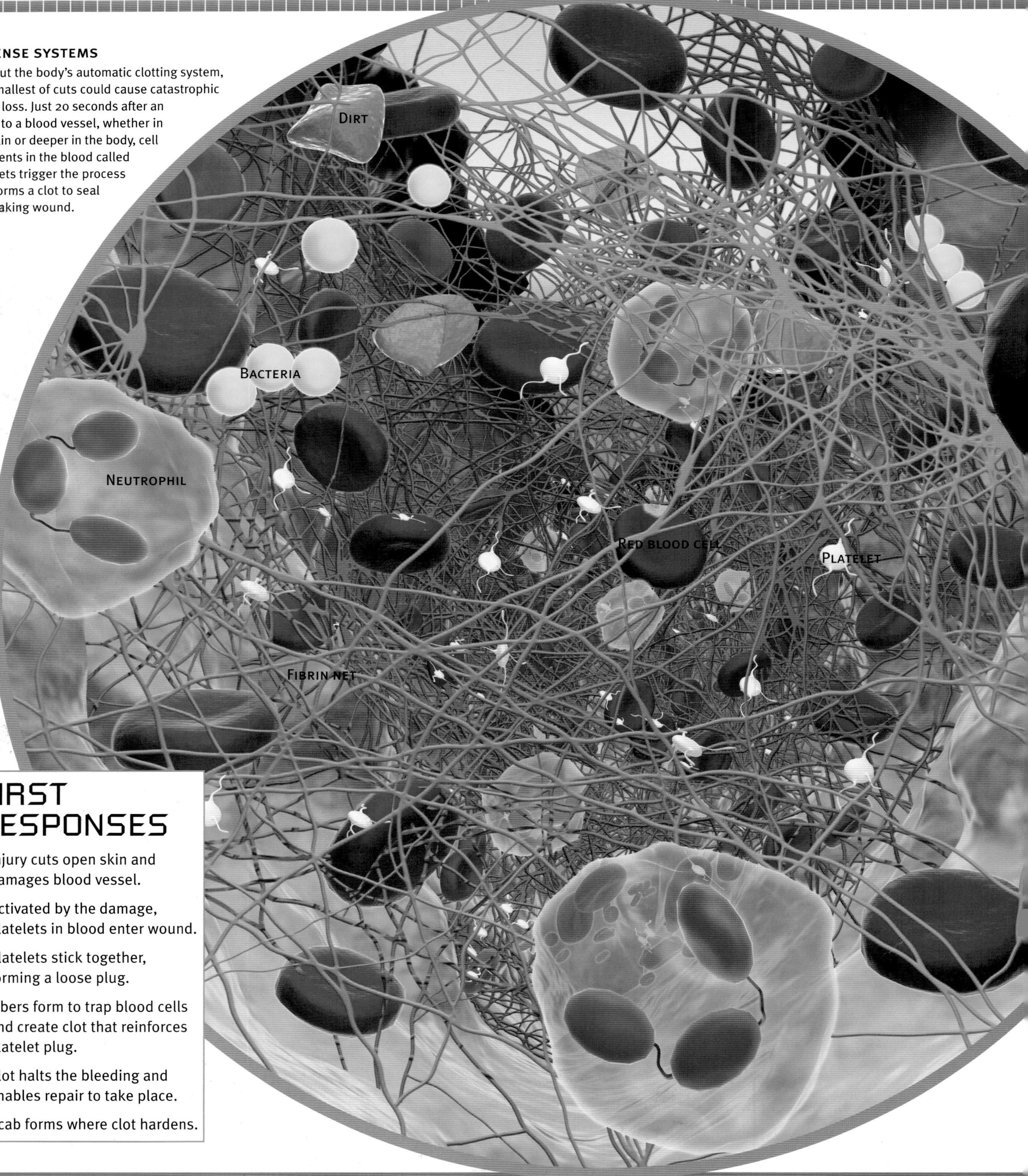

DIRT

BACTERIA

NEUTROPHIL

RED BLOOD CELL

PLATELET

FIBRIN NET

FIRST RESPONSES

- Injury cuts open skin and damages blood vessel.

- Activated by the damage, platelets in blood enter wound.

- Platelets stick together, forming a loose plug.

- Fibers form to trap blood cells and create clot that reinforces platelet plug.

- Clot halts the bleeding and enables repair to take place.

- Scab forms where clot hardens.

DATA SEARCH

- In total there are about 1,500 billion (1,500,000,000,000) platelets circulating in the 1 gallon (5 liters) of blood inside the average body.

- Fly maggots were once used to help wound healing. Some doctors are starting to use this method again because maggots eat dead tissue and bacteria in wounds, but avoid healthy, living tissue.

- People who suffer from an inherited condition called hemophilia lack one of the clotting factors, so their blood is unable to clot properly.

- Draculin, the anticoagulant (clot-preventing substance) found in the saliva of the blood-feeding vampire bat, is used as a drug to treat people at risk of heart attacks that are the result of rogue clots blocking blood vessels supplying the heart.

- Blood-sucking leeches cut through a victim's skin, releasing saliva containing hirudin, an anticoagulant. This stops clotting, so leeches enjoy an uninterrupted blood feast.

1 »

Neutrophil
This type of white blood cell tracks down and eats invading bacteria.

2 »

Activated platelets
Play a key role in clotting and preventing blood loss.

DESTROYING INVADERS

A breach in the skin allows bacteria from the outside to enter. This bacteria can potentially cause disease. While blood leaking from a broken vessel fills the wound, white blood cells being carried along in the bloodstream hunt down these invaders before obliterating them.

PLUGGING THE LEAK

Damage to the vessel triggers a change in the blood's platelets leaking into the wound. They suddenly swell, producing spiky offshoots that start sticking to each other, as well as the affected area. As platelet "plugs" form, blood loss from the wound and the pierced blood vessel is greatly reduced.

3 »

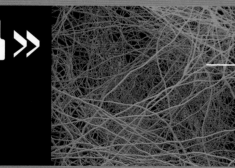

Fibrin net
Formed when long fibrin threads trap blood cells.

4 »

Edges of wound
Drawn together when platelets contract.

CLOTTING THE BLOOD

Sticky platelets also activate chemicals in the blood called clotting factors. These convert a soluble blood protein called fibrinogen into long, insoluble threads of fibrin. The threads form a meshwork, similar to a fishing net. By trapping blood cells within the net, liquid blood turns into a gel-like clot that halts bleeding.

PULLING TOGETHER

About 30 minutes after the injury has occurred, the platelets contract (shrink) and tug on the fibrin net. This has the effect of pulling the edges of the wound closer together. The platelets then release chemicals that stimulate cells to divide and start repairing the damage.

SCAB PROTECTION

This magnified (x 390) view of the skin (brown) shows a scab (red) covering a five-day-old wound. A scab consists of a mixture of dried, clotted blood and dead skin cells. It forms a hard crust that seals the upper part of the wound, protecting the damaged skin and blood vessels beneath it as they repair themselves. The scab also keeps out harmful bacteria. Picking scabs should be avoided because of the risks of undoing repairs and causing infection. Eventually the scab falls off, revealing brand new skin.

EVAPORATION

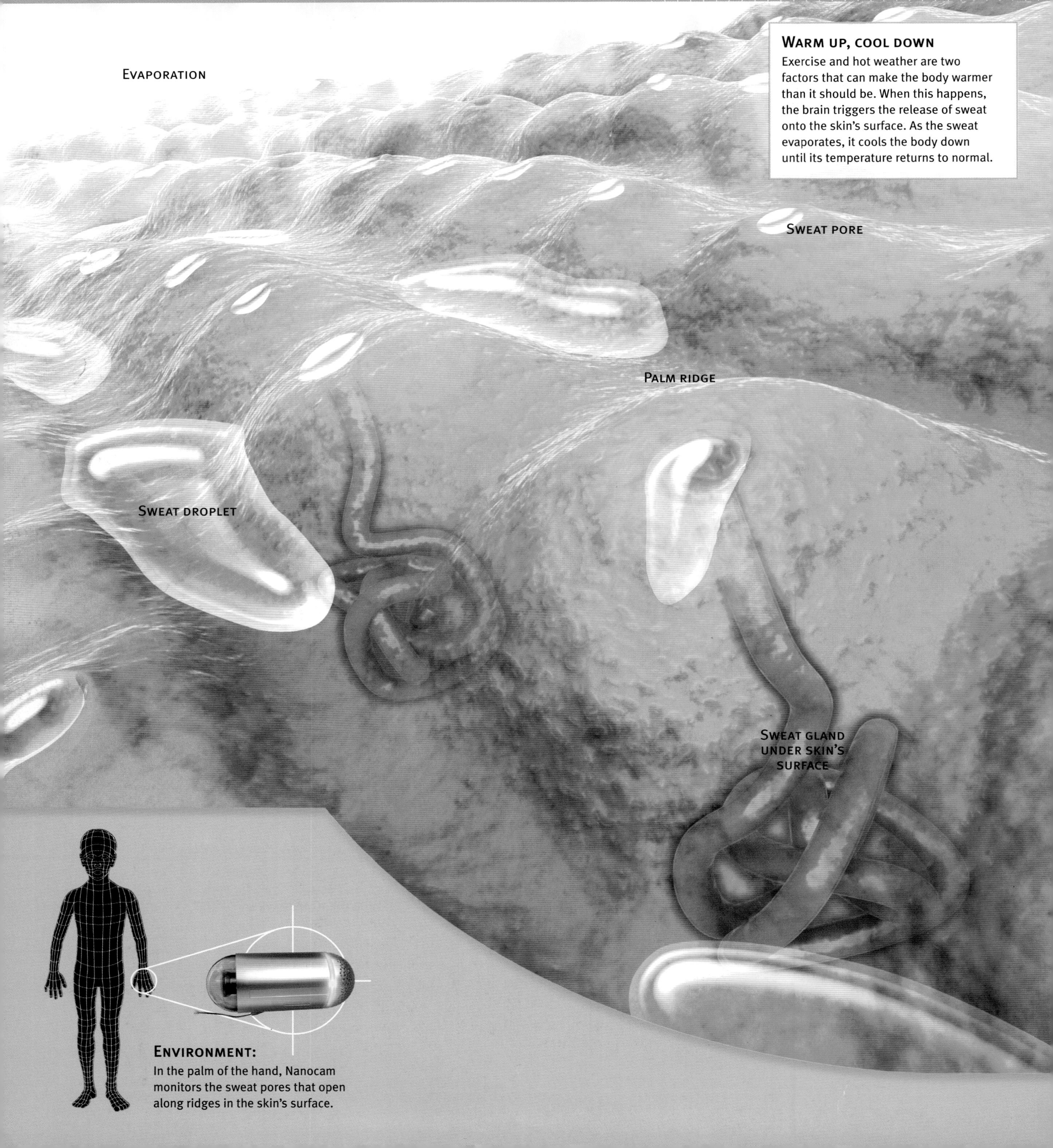

WARM UP, COOL DOWN
Exercise and hot weather are two factors that can make the body warmer than it should be. When this happens, the brain triggers the release of sweat onto the skin's surface. As the sweat evaporates, it cools the body down until its temperature returns to normal.

SWEAT PORE

PALM RIDGE

SWEAT DROPLET

SWEAT GLAND UNDER SKIN'S SURFACE

ENVIRONMENT:
In the palm of the hand, Nanocam monitors the sweat pores that open along ridges in the skin's surface.

TEMPERATURE CONTROL

Your internal body temperature must stay around 98.6°F (37°C), regardless of how hot or cold the outside temperature is, or how active you are. If your body temperature rises or falls, cells and tissues stop working normally and you become unwell. Sweating plays a vital part in the automatic mechanism that keeps body temperature constant.

FIRST RESPONSES

- A hot day raises your body and blood temperature.

- This rise is detected by the hypothalamus, part of the brain.

- Hypothalamus sends nerve messages to sweat glands, triggering increased sweat production to cool the body.

- Feel wetness of sweat on the skin's surface.

1 »

Sweat duct
Short tube carrying sweat to skin's surface.

Sweat gland
Coiled structure located in dermis of skin.

2 »

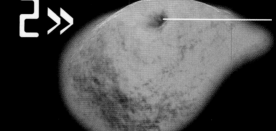

Sweat pore
Funnel-shaped opening of sweat duct.

PRODUCTION LINE

Sweat glands in the skin make sweat, and the level of production steps up when the body gets too hot. Each individual gland consists of coiled tubes lined with gland cells. Water and salts are filtered through these cells from the bloodstream, which flows along in capillaries surrounding the gland.

SWEAT IT OUT

Whenever the body's core temperature goes up, the extra sweat produced by each sweat gland passes along a short duct before emptying onto the surface of the skin through an opening called a sweat pore. Altogether, there are nearly three million pores in the skin ready to release sweat in the body's mission to cool itself down.

3 »

Sweat
Watery liquid produced by sweat glands.

4 »

Water vapor
As sweat evaporates, molecules of water pass into the air.

SOGGY SURFACE

As sweat exits pores all over the palm, it spreads out, running down the ridges and into the grooves, creating a clammy feel to the touch. Sweat is about 99 percent water. Body salts are also dissolved in the water and this is why sweat tastes salty. Tiny amounts of waste, such as urea, a component of urine, make up the rest of the sweat mix.

EVAPORATION

Using heat from the body, water molecules near the surface of the sweat layer gain enough energy to escape into the air as a gas called water vapor. This is the process of evaporation, in which heat is removed from the skin's surface and its blood vessels. As the blood's temperature falls, sweating decreases and the body temperature returns to normal.

DATA SEARCH

- Sweat glands are most abundant on the forehead, palms, and soles, but absent from the lips and nipples.

- The body loses about 1 cup (200 ml) of sweat a day, but this increases to just over a quart (1 liter) per hour in hot conditions.

- If body temperature rises, the brain also triggers widening of the skin blood vessels so extra heat can be released outside.

- Sweat evaporation slows down by a lot in humid weather, leaving people hot, uncomfortable, and soaked in sweat.

- Sweat glands in the armpits become active at puberty, producing a thicker sweat that, when broken down by bacteria, can create a strong smell.

- Feelings of fear or strong emotions can also result in sweating.

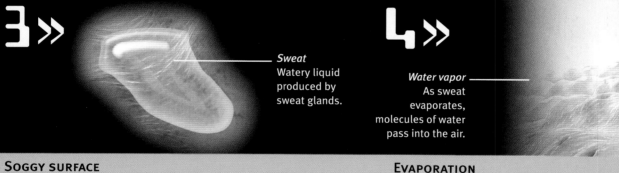
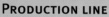

BODY BUGS

Skin can provide a home for many kinds of microscopic animals. These body bugs are parasites that can live and feed on us, often causing irritation.

Some, such as scabies mites and chiggers, are mites, close relatives of spiders. Others, such as head lice and fleas, are wingless insects with flattened bodies. Thanks to these adaptations, they move easily between body hairs. Parasites live on the skin, so they avoid the body's natural defenses. As a result, bug-killing creams or shampoos are often needed to eliminate them. Dust mites are not parasites but can affect human health.

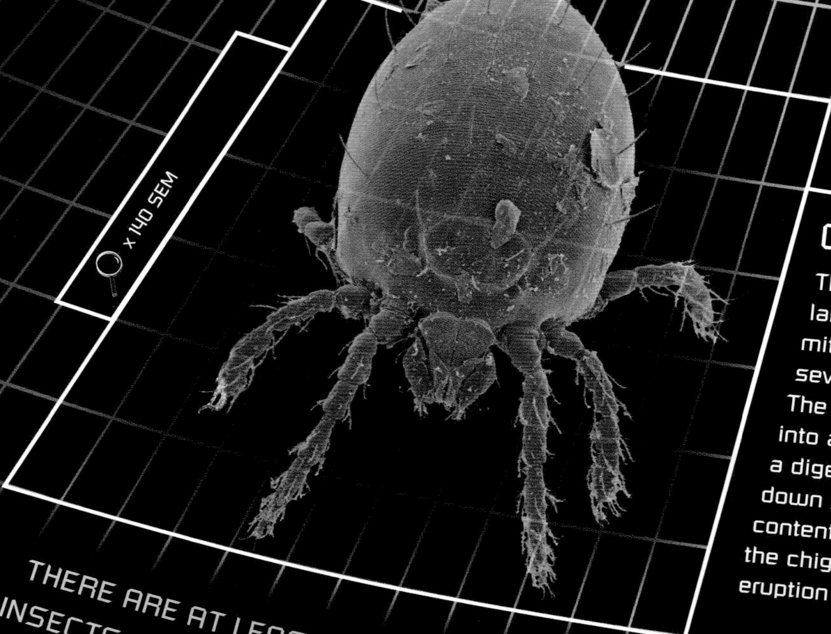

x 140 SEM

CHIGGER

Though tiny, this six-legged larva of a harmless harvest mite is often the cause of severe itching in summer. The chigger sticks its head into a hair follicle and releases a digestive fluid. This breaks down skin cells, so that their contents can be sucked up by the chigger. It also triggers the eruption of very itchy red pimples.

THERE ARE AT LEAST TEN QUINTILLION (TEN MILLION TRILLION) INSECTS ON EARTH, COMPARED WITH ONLY SIX BILLION HUMANS.

DUST MITE

A million microscopic dust mites just like this one are lurking in your bed. They feed on the thousands of dead skin flakes that fall from your body every minute. These flakes form a major part of household dust. If breathed in, the droppings of dust mites can trigger asthma attacks in some people.

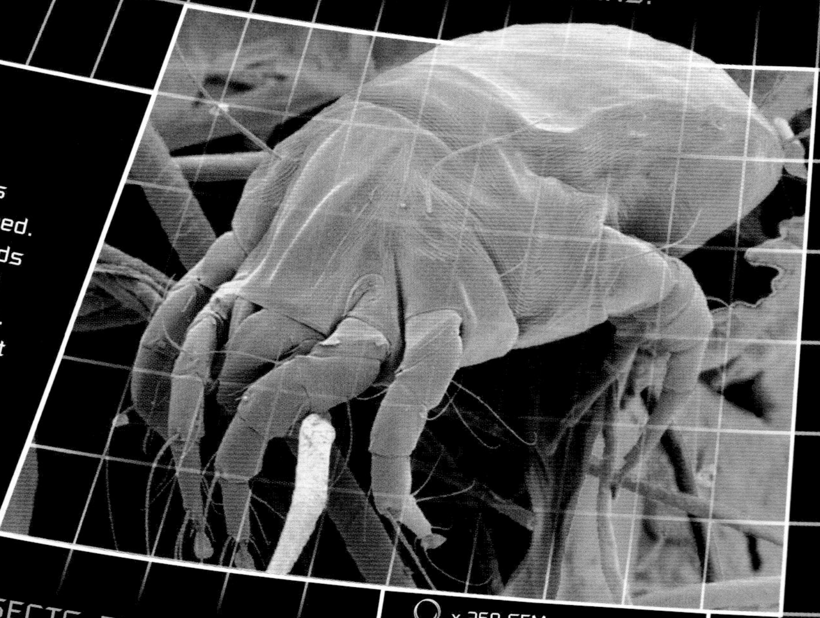

THERE ARE 900,000 NAMED SPECIES (TYPES) OF INSECTS, BUT IT IS THOUGHT THERE ARE ABOUT 30 MILLION SPECIES ALTOGETHER.

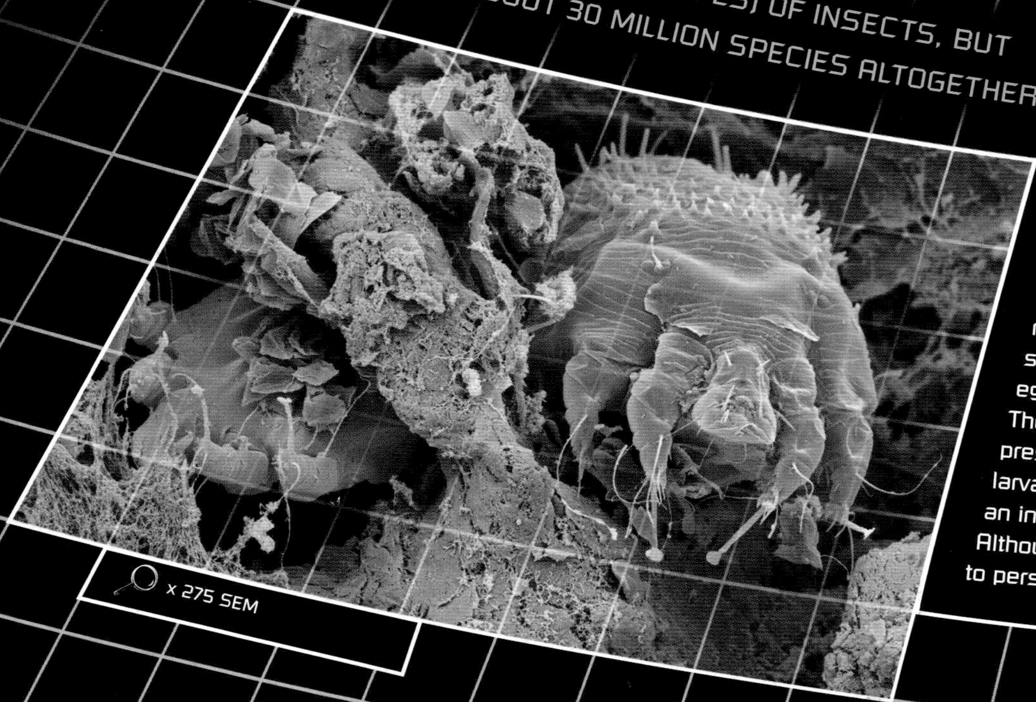

x 260 SEM

SCABIES MITE

Nicknamed the itch mite, the minuscule female scabies mite uses her piercing mouth to excavate a tunnel under the skin. In this newly dug burrow she lays eggs that soon hatch into larval mites. The combination of burrowing and the presence of mite droppings, saliva, and larvae severely irritate the skin. Scabies— an intense, maddening itching—results. Although scabies passes easily from person to person, it can be treated with skin lotions.

x 275 SEM

x 100 SEM

SOME INSECTS AND
MITES CAN CARRY
AND SPREAD SERIOUS
DISEASES INCLUDING
MALARIA, SLEEPING
SICKNESS, AND TYPHUS.

INSECTS LIVE VIRTUALLY EVERYWHERE, EXCEPT IN THE SEA, WHEREAS MITES ARE FOUND IN EVERY TYPE OF HABITAT.

HEAD LOUSE

This sesame seed-sized head louse is using its curved claws to grip tightly to a hair. Itchy head lice are common among children, and travel from one child's head to another when they touch. The louse pierces the scalp, injects an anticoagulant— which stops blood from clotting but causes itching— and feeds on the blood. Head lice are removed with nit combs or special shampoo.

TICKS ARE RELATIVES OF MITES—THEY SWELL UP LIKE BALLOONS AS THEY FEED ON BLOOD, BEFORE DROPPING OFF TO DIGEST THEIR MEALS.

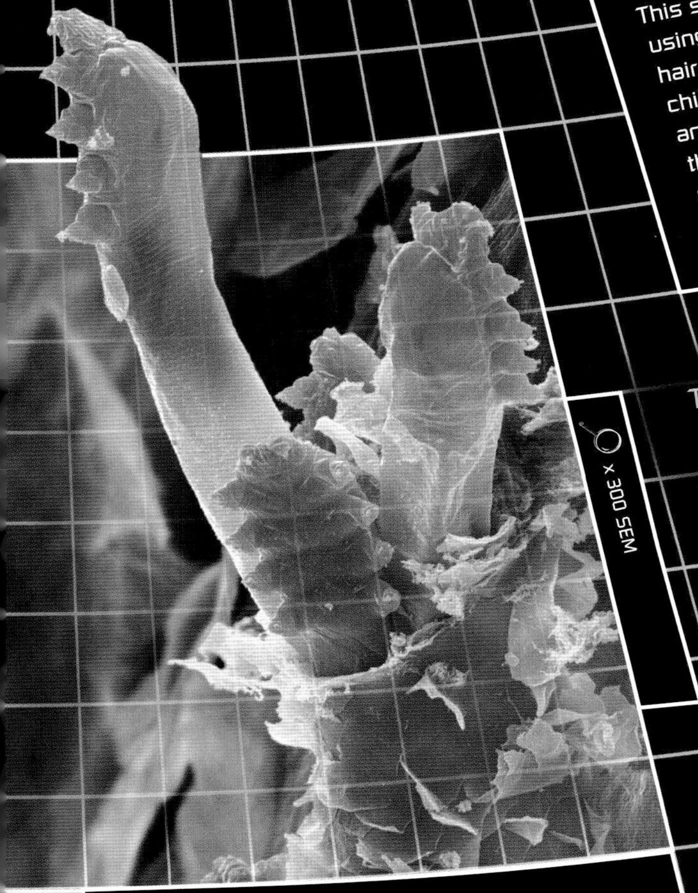

x 300 SEM

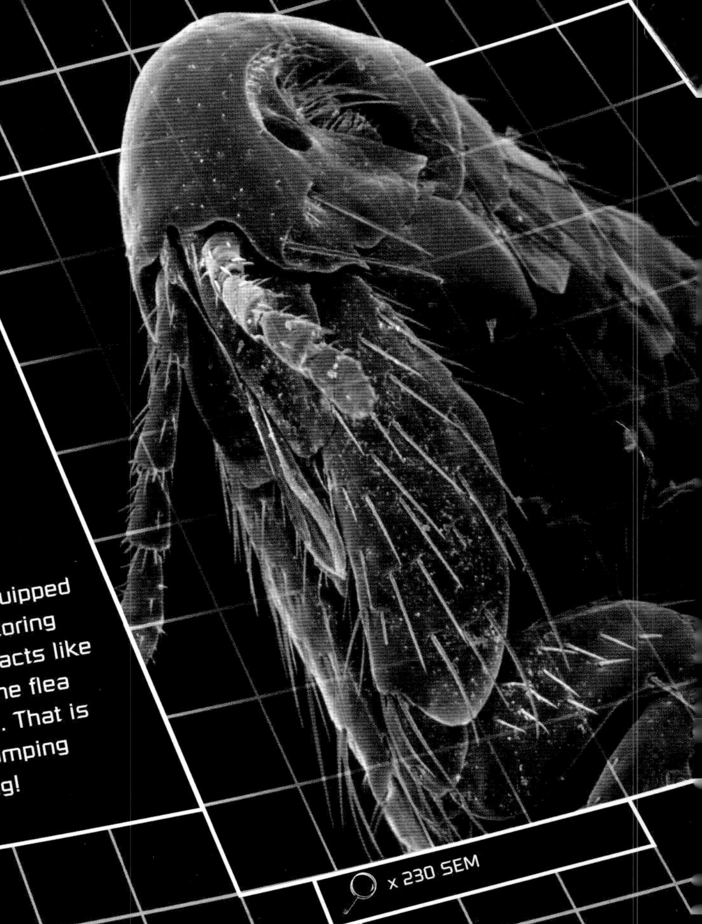

FLEA

This is the head of a cat flea— an insect that pierces the skin and feeds on the blood of both cats and humans. Fleas only remain on their host when feeding and rely on jumping to get from one meal to the next. Their hind legs are equipped with the elastic, energy-storing substance resilin, which acts like a bowstring, launching the flea into a 12-in (30-cm) leap. That is the equivalent of you jumping over a 60-story building!

EYELASH MITE

Here, several sausage-shaped eyelash mites project out of a hair follicle from which an eyelash grows. It may come as a shock to learn that just about everyone, usually unknowingly, has eyelash mites. They are far too small to be noticed, even if you stare into a mirror. The good news is that eyelash mites do not cause any harm. They simply stay squeezed inside the hair follicles, feeding on your dead skin cells and oily secretions from the sebaceous glands.

x 230 SEM

HOT WATER

MEDIAN NERVE

SENSORY NEURONS
INSIDE NERVE

NERVE IMPULSE

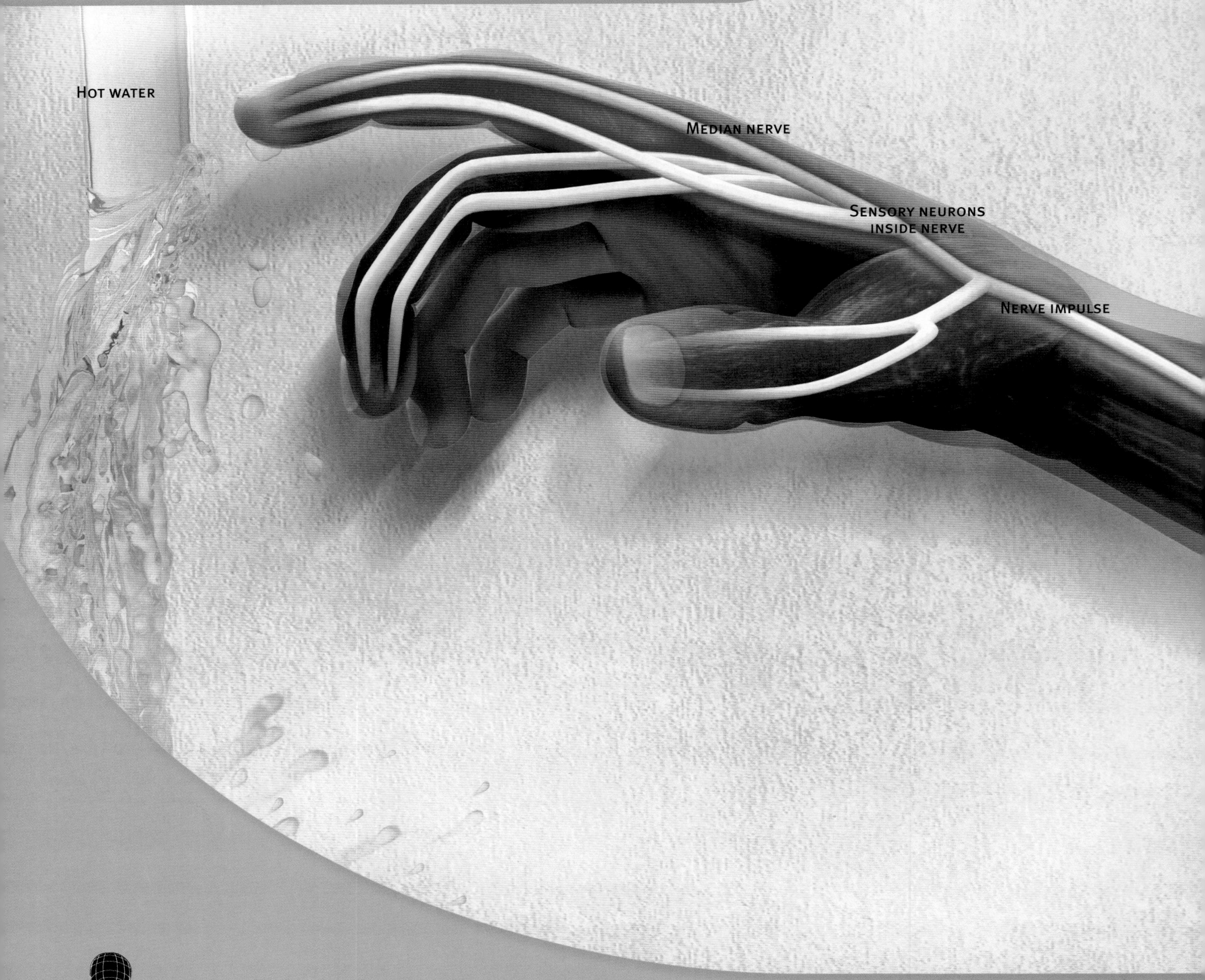

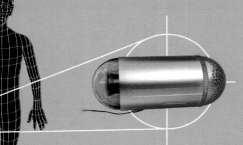

ENVIRONMENT:
Emergency indicator flashing red, Nanocam
follows the split-second reaction as the
body keeps from scalding.

AUTOMATIC REACTION

A withdrawal reflex pulls a body
part away from danger before
the brain has time to think about
it. Here, the hand is threatened
with very hot water. A high-speed
message travels from the hand
via the spinal cord to the upper
arm muscle, which pulls the hand
away. Only afterward does the
brain respond, and pain is felt.

HOT WATER
Running water straight from the
hot faucet can be far hotter than
expected, with the potential
to badly scald the skin of
the fingers.

SKIN
Receptors in the skin are
responsible for detecting heat
and pain. When very hot water hits
the skin's surface, receptors react
by generating nerve impulses.

MUSCULOCUTANEOUS
NERVE

MOTOR
NEURONS
INSIDE NERVE

BICEPS BRACHII
MUSCLE

NERVE IMPULSES
These tiny electrical signals travel along the nervous system's neurons (nerve cells). Outside the brain and spinal cord, neurons are bundled in cablelike nerves.

SENSORY NEURONS
Sensory neurons are nerve cells relaying nerve impulses from skin receptors to the central nervous system (CNS)—the spinal cord and the brain.

MEDIAN NERVE
This nerve runs down the arm to the hand. It contains sensory neurons that link receptors in the skin of the fingers to the spinal cord muscles.

MOTOR NEURONS
These neurons relay nerve impulses from the CNS to muscles. They are bundled in the musculocutaneous nerve linking the spinal cord to the biceps brachii.

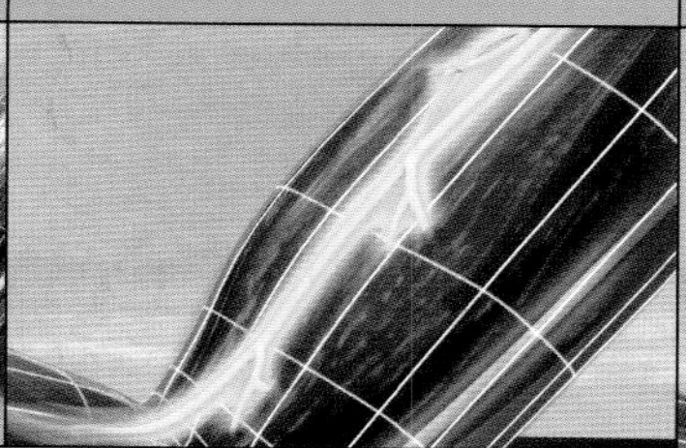

BICEPS BRACHII MUSCLE
On receiving the nerve message from the spinal cord, the biceps brachii muscle contracts, immediately pulling the hand away from the scalding water.

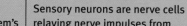

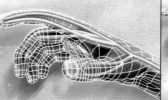

NANOCAM REPORT: REFLEX ACTION

Defense systems

Always ready for action, withdrawal reflexes pull a body part away from danger instantly. In a reflex action, nerve impulses travel along neurons from skin receptor to muscle via the spinal cord. The end of a neuron forms a junction with muscle fibers. When nerve impulses cross the junction, the muscle contracts.

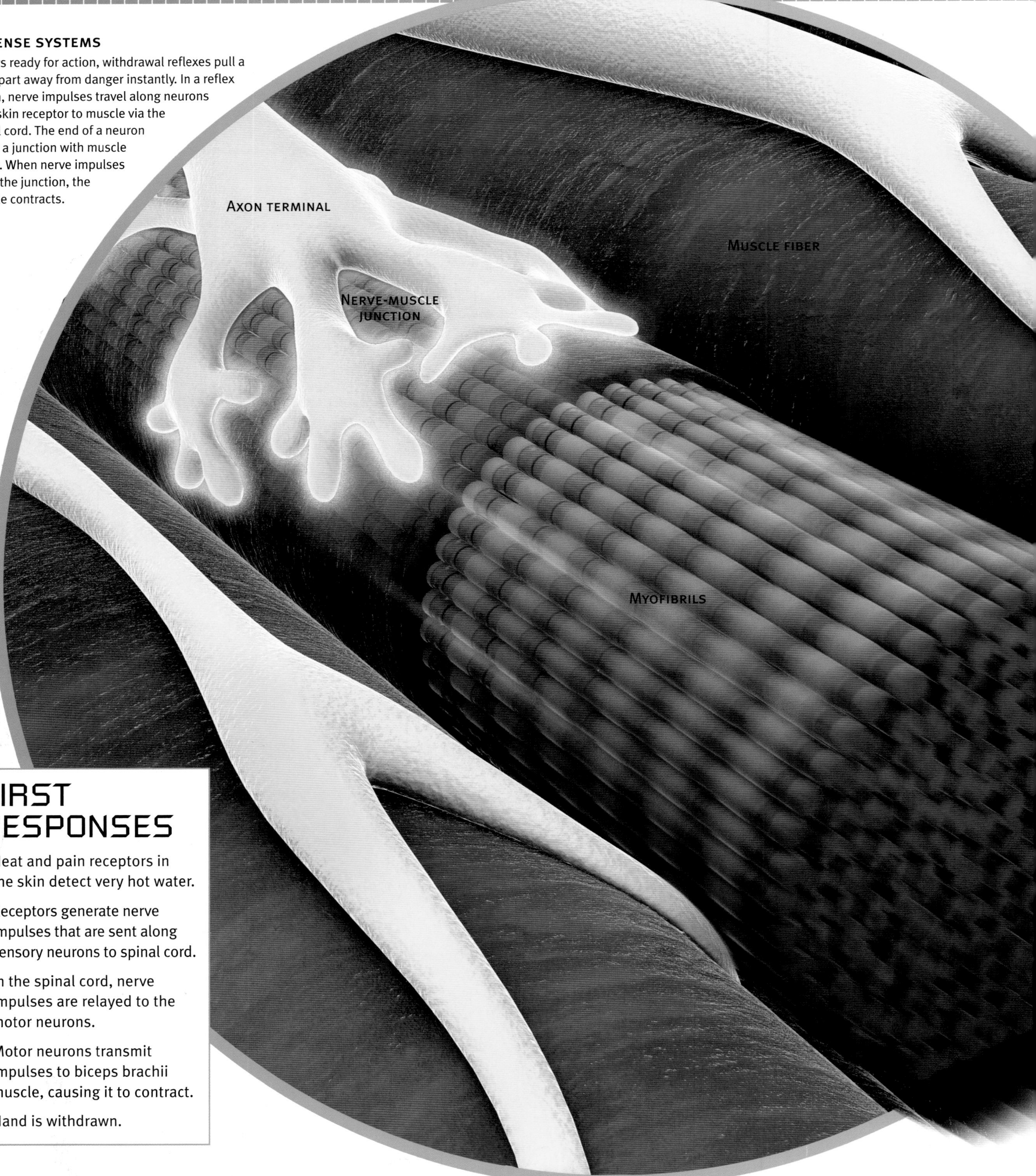

Axon terminal
Muscle fiber
Nerve-muscle junction
Myofibrils

FIRST RESPONSES

- Heat and pain receptors in the skin detect very hot water.
- Receptors generate nerve impulses that are sent along sensory neurons to spinal cord.
- In the spinal cord, nerve impulses are relayed to the motor neurons.
- Motor neurons transmit impulses to biceps brachii muscle, causing it to contract.
- Hand is withdrawn.

DATA SEARCH

- The hand withdrawal reflex takes just 0.01 seconds (10 milliseconds) because nerve impulses can travel along neurons at an incredible 330 ft per second (100 m per second).

- There are more than 650 skeletal muscles in the body (including the biceps brachii) and these make up to 40 percent of the body's mass. This body mass percentage is even higher in bodybuilders, because of the exaggerated size of their muscles.

- At its widest point, the spinal cord is as thick as a finger. It gives rise to 31 pairs of branching spinal nerves that carry both sensory and motor neurons. These extend to all parts of the body.

- Newborn babies have "built-in" reflexes that aid their survival. These include rooting (finding their mother's milk supply) and, if immersed in water, automatically holding their breath and making swimming movements. These reflexes disappear in the first year of life.

1 »

Axon terminal
One of the branches at the end of the axon (nerve fiber) of a motor neuron.

2 »

Nerve-muscle junction
Place where an axon terminal meets a muscle fiber

NERVE IMPULSES ARRIVE

Bundled inside each nerve are the long axons, or nerve fibers, of motor neurons. These extend from the spinal cord to the biceps muscle in the arm and carry the tiny electrical signals called nerve impulses. When the axon reaches a muscle it divides into flattened branches called axon terminals, each serving its own muscle fiber.

BRIDGING THE GAP

Inside the nerve-muscle junction, the axon terminal and the membrane (surface) of the muscle fiber are separated by a tiny gap called a synapse. When a nerve impulse arrives at the axon terminal it triggers the release of a chemical, known as a neurotransmitter, which travels across the synapse to the membrane of the muscle fiber.

3 »

Muscle fiber
One of the many long, cylindrical cells that makes up a skeletal muscle.

4 »

Myofibrils
Rodlike, parallel structures that fill a muscle fiber.

MASS IMPULSE

When the neurotransmitter "hits" the muscle fiber membrane it triggers a new impulse, which passes along through the fiber. The muscle is made up of bundles of fibers, and each fiber is served by an axon terminal. This means that, during a reflex action, impulses are traveling into many muscle fibers at the same time.

FINAL CONTRACTION

Inside each muscle fiber is an arrangement of myofibrils that contract (get shorter) when a nerve impulse arrives. As the myofibrils shorten, so do the muscle fibers, and the muscle contracts. If more neurons "fire," more fibers shorten and the contraction is stronger. Glucose and oxygen, delivered by the blood, supply the energy for contraction.

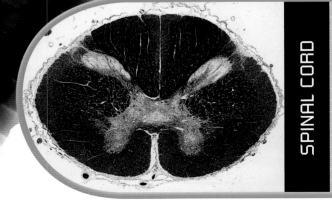

SPINAL CORD

Extending down the back from the brain, the spinal cord relays messages between brain and body, and is involved in many reflexes. This is a cross-section through the spinal cord, with the back of the spinal cord at the top. The butterfly-shaped gray matter (yellow here) contains neurons that, during the withdrawal reflex, relay nerve impulses from sensory neurons (enter gray matter at the back) to motor neurons (exit gray matter at the front). White matter (black here) contains nerve fibers that relay signals to and from the brain.

PAIN RECEPTOR

HAIR FOLLICLE

NERVE FIBER

VEIN

ARTERY

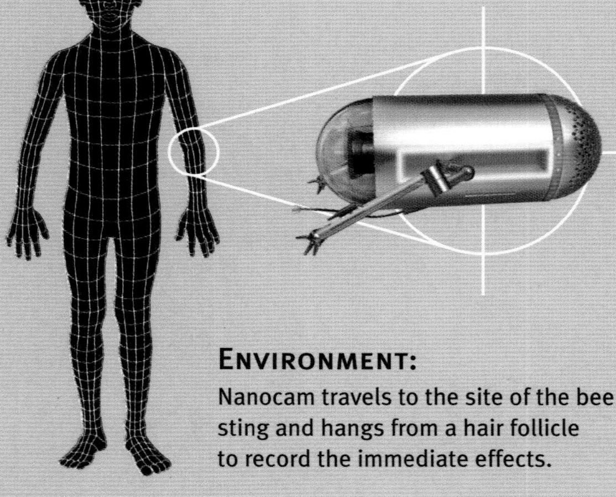

UNDER ATTACK

Skin provides your body with a strong, protective layer. When your skin comes under attack, pain receptors send a warning message to the brain. In the event of a major threat, such as skin being pierced and bee venom injected, your defense systems also kick in. The result is all-out chemical warfare.

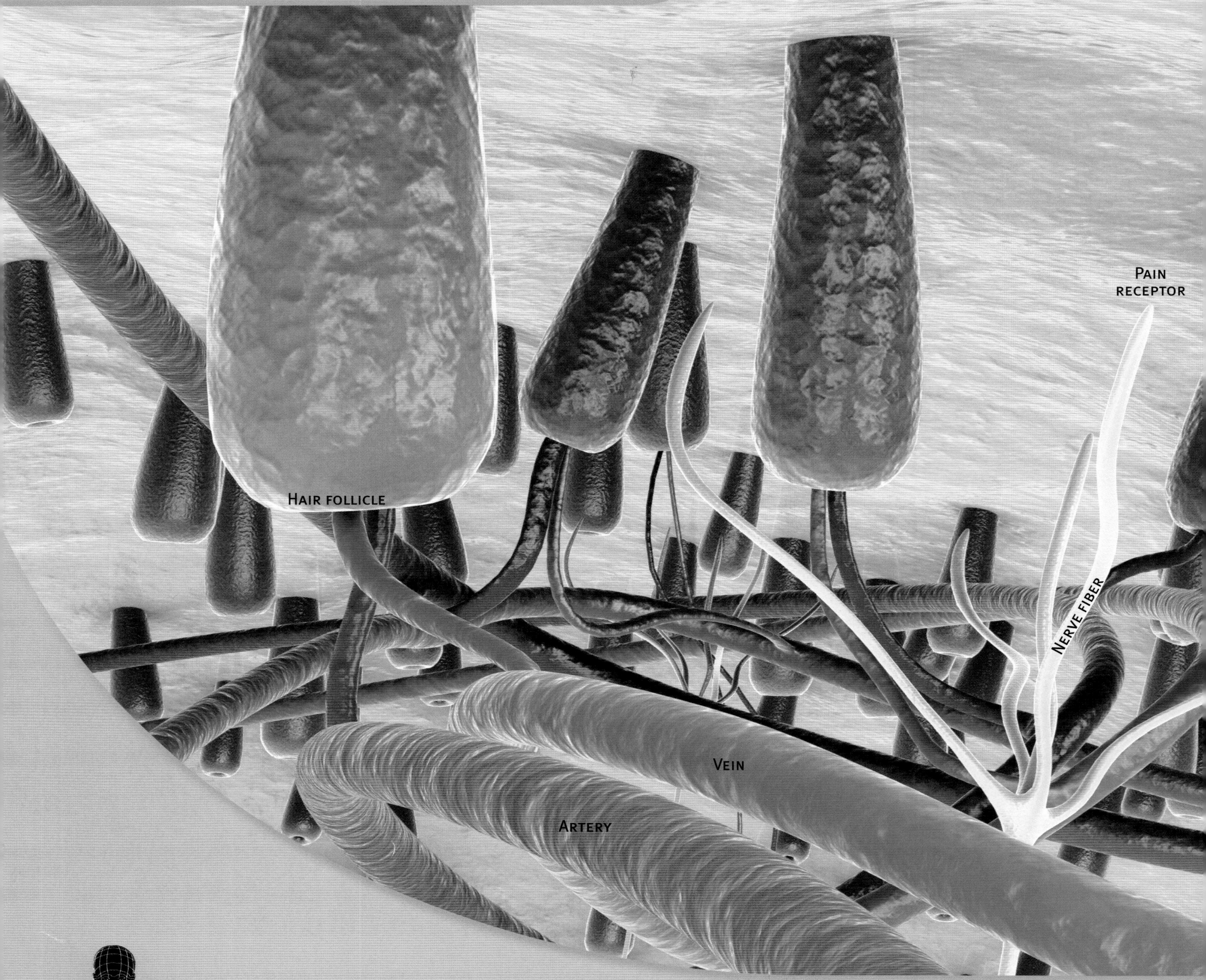

ENVIRONMENT:
Nanocam travels to the site of the bee sting and hangs from a hair follicle to record the immediate effects.

BEE STING
The sting saws away at the skin, while a venom sac in the abdomen pumps in chemicals. The sting and the sac stay in the wound, ripped from the bee as it flies away.

HAIR FOLLICLE
Each of your body hairs grows from a follicle—a deep "bag" that extends down from the skin's surface. Body hair is too short to prevent the bee from inserting its sting.

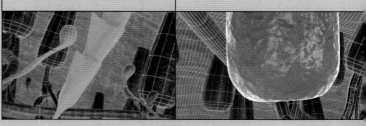

EPIDERMIS

BEE ABDOMEN

INFLAMMATION

BEE STING

EPIDERMIS
The scalpel-sharp point of the sting cuts through this top layer of skin, as easily as a hot knife through butter. Once punctured, the epidermis allows marauding germs to enter.

PAIN RECEPTOR
Dotted under your skin's surface are pain receptors—nerve endings that respond to the dangerous tearing action of the sting and the potent poisons in the bee venom.

NERVE FIBER
Pain receptors detect the sting and trigger nerve impulses that travel at high speed along tiny cables called nerve fibers to the brain. This is when you feel pain.

BLOOD VESSELS
Arteries carry oxygen-rich blood to the skin, while veins return oxygen-poor blood to your heart. After the sting, arteries widen to increase blood flow to the wound.

INFLAMMATION
Redness, swelling, and itchiness are your body's responses to being stung. Extra blood brings germ-killers and healing properties, and dilutes the bee venom.

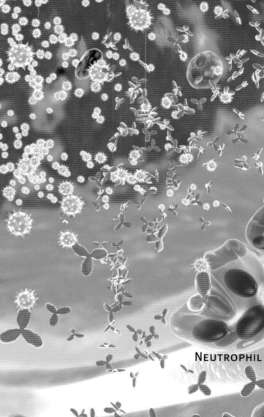

FIRST RESPONSES

- Urgent message sent from brain to finger muscles to remove bee sting immediately.

- Sting then scraped or flicked out with a fingernail.

- Immune (defense) system activated to fight the invading venom.

- Skin around the sting site washed with soap and water.

- An ice pack applied to keep the sting site cool.

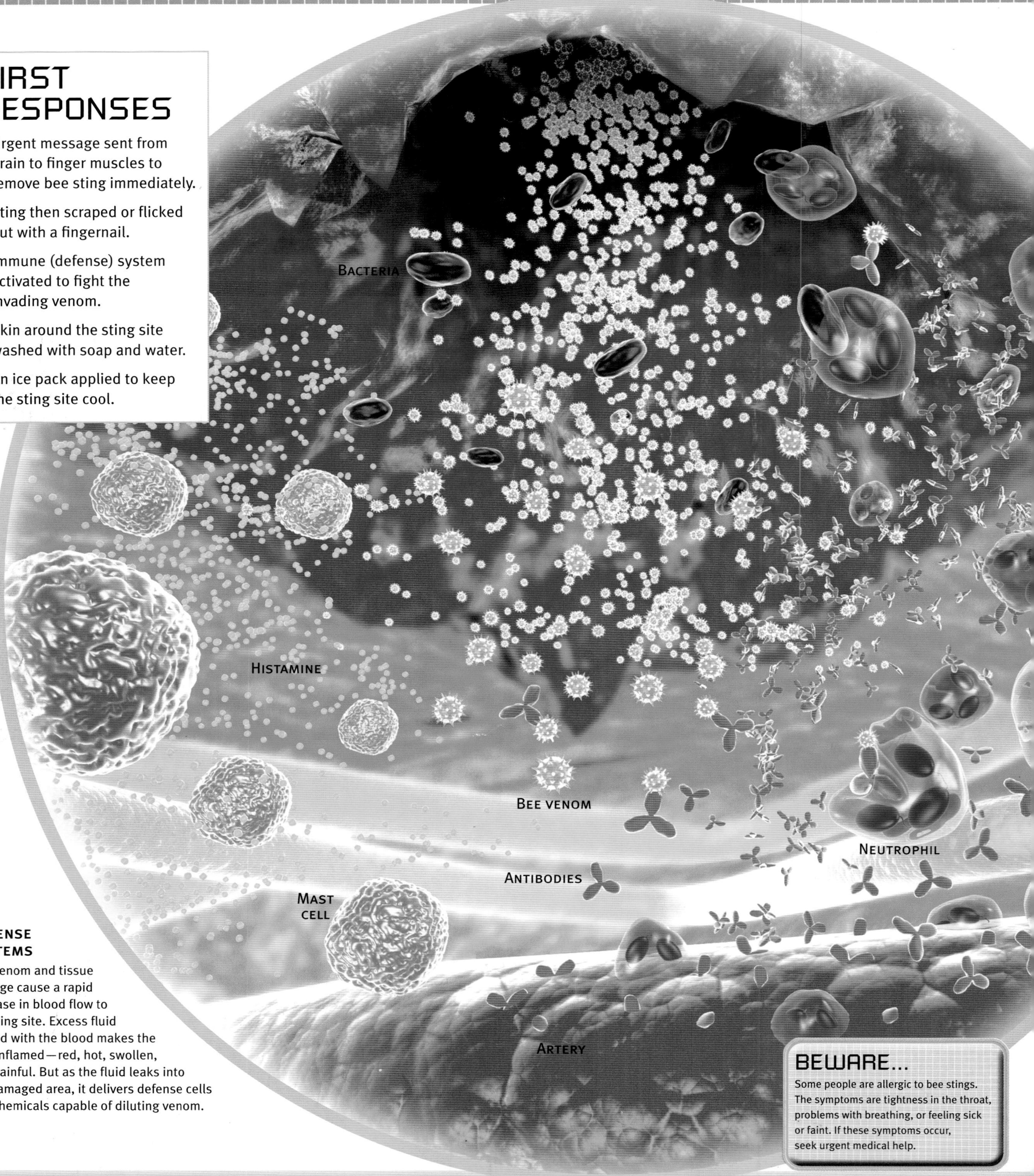

BACTERIA

HISTAMINE

BEE VENOM

NEUTROPHIL

ANTIBODIES

MAST CELL

ARTERY

DEFENSE SYSTEMS

Bee venom and tissue damage cause a rapid increase in blood flow to the sting site. Excess fluid carried with the blood makes the skin inflamed—red, hot, swollen, and painful. But as the fluid leaks into the damaged area, it delivers defense cells and chemicals capable of diluting venom.

BEWARE...

Some people are allergic to bee stings. The symptoms are tightness in the throat, problems with breathing, or feeling sick or faint. If these symptoms occur, seek urgent medical help.

DATA SEARCH

- A bee's warning pheromones smell a little like dirty socks. So, to keep from being stung, beekeepers often wash and change into clean clothes before visiting their hives.

- Bees are important in nature. As they collect nectar, they transfer pollen from flower to flower so that plants can make seeds and reproduce.

- A bee dies when it stings you because the sting and venom sac are ripped from its body. A wasp's sting is smooth, so it can sting you again and again.

- Some alternative therapists believe that bee venom can help people with painful arthritis. They deliberately sting the affected joint in an attempt to reduce pain, swelling, and redness.

1 >>

Venom
Poison used by some animals for defense or to stun prey.

2 >>

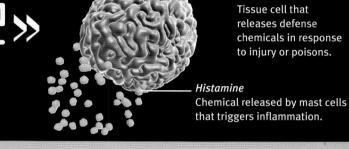

Mast cell
Tissue cell that releases defense chemicals in response to injury or poisons.

Histamine
Chemical released by mast cells that triggers inflammation.

INVASION OF VENOM

At the point where the bee stings, its barbed sting saws into the skin. Simultaneously, poisonous liquid venom is pumped from the bee's venom sac directly into the open wound. Harmful substances in the venom cause immediate pain and damage tissue.

BLOOD ARMY AT WORK

Tissue damage and the toxic effects of bee venom cause the immune system's mast cells to release a chemical called histamine. This makes blood vessels wider and leakier, allowing an increased flow of blood and more neutrophils and antibodies to reach the tissue of the sting site.

3 >>

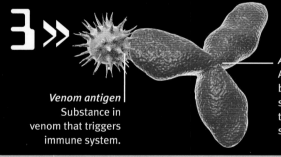

Venom antigen
Substance in venom that triggers immune system.

Antibody
A protein produced by the immune system that binds to specific problem substances.

4 >>

Neutrophil
Most common type of white blood cell.

Bacteria and venom antigen
Invaders are swallowed by neutrophils.

ATTACK OF THE ANTIBODIES

When the bee venom is detected, the body's immune system releases chemicals called antibodies that have Y-shaped molecules. These are carried by the blood to the sting site where they specifically target bee venom. They lock onto venom antigens and stop the venom from working.

HUNGRY NEUTROPHILS EAT INVADERS

Newly joined antibodies and venom antigens are targeted and eaten by neutrophils. But sting damage also lets in bacteria from the skin's surface. These will multiply and release toxins that cause infection. Luckily, neutrophils attracted to the sting site hunt, engulf, and eat bacteria. The clean-up operation is now complete.

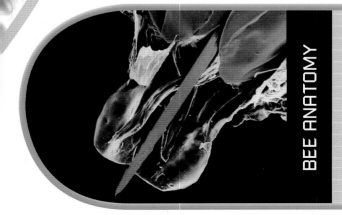

BEE ANATOMY

This magnified (x 17.5) image of the rear end of a honeybee shows part of its stinging anatomy, including the barbed, needlelike sting. When a bee stings someone, muscles push and pull the sting so it saws its way into the skin. During the stinging process, the sting is ripped from the bee, together with the venom-filled sac and attached muscles. The barbs keep on working the sting deep into the skin, as venom is pumped inside the wound.

UV RAYS

EPIDERMIS

KERATINOCYTE

MELANIN
GRANULES

MELANOCYTE

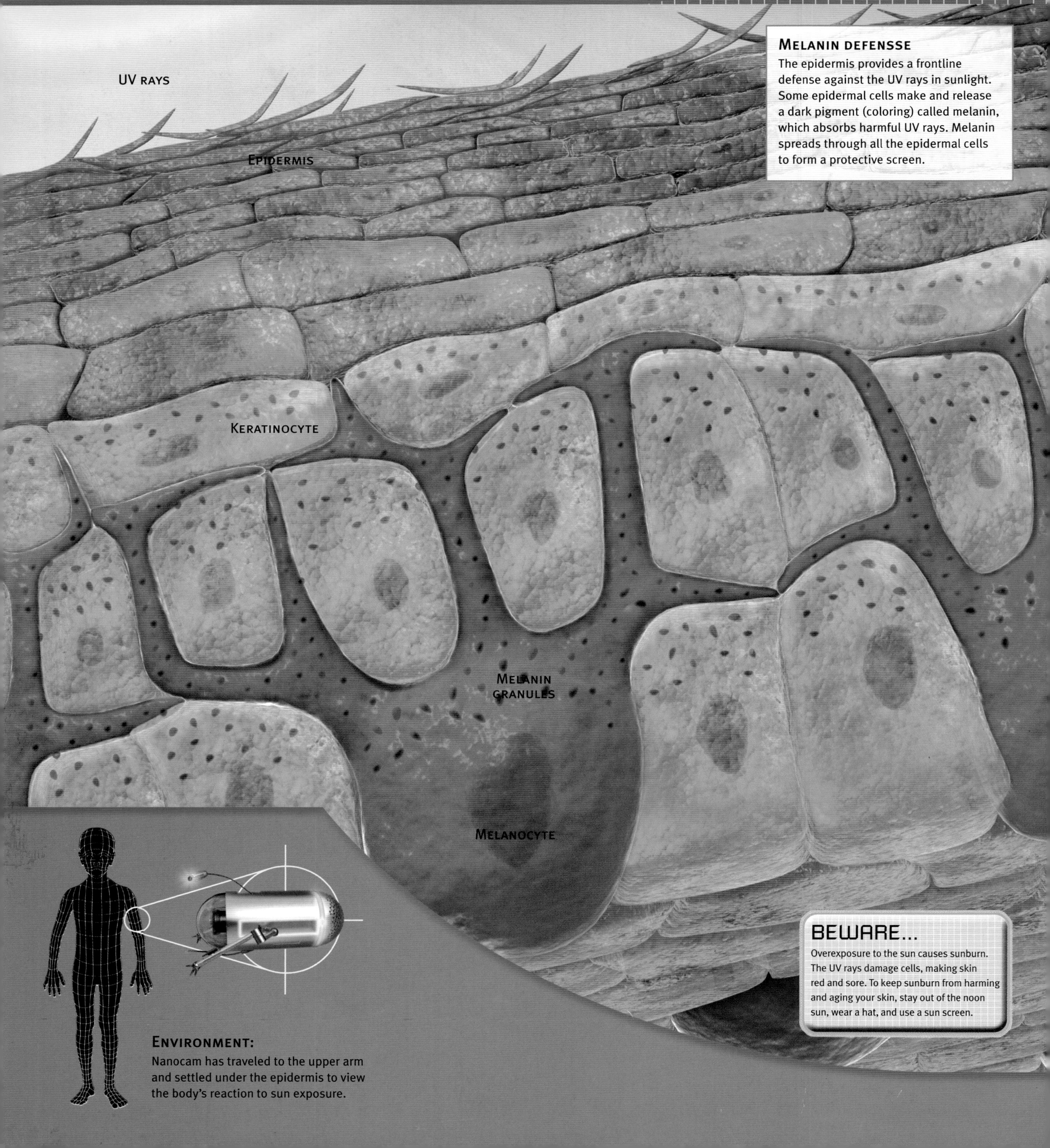

MELANIN DEFENSSE

The epidermis provides a frontline defense against the UV rays in sunlight. Some epidermal cells make and release a dark pigment (coloring) called melanin, which absorbs harmful UV rays. Melanin spreads through all the epidermal cells to form a protective screen.

BEWARE...

Overexposure to the sun causes sunburn. The UV rays damage cells, making skin red and sore. To keep sunburn from harming and aging your skin, stay out of the noon sun, wear a hat, and use a sun screen.

ENVIRONMENT:

Nanocam has traveled to the upper arm and settled under the epidermis to view the body's reaction to sun exposure.

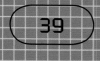

SUNLIGHT ON SKIN

Light from the Sun is made up of visible light you can see, infrared rays that keep you warm, and ultraviolet (UV) rays. UV rays are potentially harmful to the skin, causing burning and wrinkles, as well as damage to the DNA (genetic instructions) inside skin cells. The epidermis, the upper layer of skin, forms a barrier around the body that helps protect us from these rays.

FIRST RESPONSES

- Feeling of increased warmth from the Sun's heat on the skin is recognized when receptors respond by sending messages to the brain.

- In defense against sunlight, the skin increases its production of the protective pigment melanin.

- Darkening of skin as melanin levels in the epidermis rise.

 1 »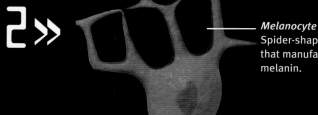

UV rays
Make up part of the radiation in sunlight.

2 »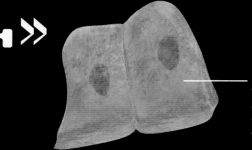

Melanocyte
Spider-shaped cell that manufactures melanin.

RAYS REACH EPIDERMIS

When sunlight hits the skin, its UV rays are able to penetrate the thin epidermis layer, passing through and between its cells. The upper layers of cells in the epidermis are dead and flattened, while the deeper ones are living. Some of these deeper cells are pigment producers called melanocytes.

MELANIN PRODUCTION STEPS UP

Inside melanocytes (their name means "black cells"), a chemical reaction takes place and the brown-black pigment melanin is produced. This contributes to the skin's natural color and, more importantly, absorbs harmful UV rays. When UV rays touch the melanocytes, the melanin goes darker than usual and its rate of production speeds up.

3 »

Melanin granules
Produced by tiny bodies called melanosomes inside melanocytes.

4 »

Keratinocytes
These general epidermal cells far outnumber the melanocytes.

MELANIN MIGRATES TO THE FRONTLINE

Triggered by the UV rays, the extra melanin is manufactured inside tiny melanin-making "bags" called melanosomes. Now packed with melanin, the melanosomes migrate along the "legs" of the melanocyte. The melanosomes pass between neighboring keratinocytes ("ordinary" epidermal cells), transferring their melanin granules into them along the way.

PROTECTIVE SCREEN IN PLACE

Inside each keratinocyte, dark melanin granules cluster to form a protective screen above the cell's nucleus (containing DNA). Keratinocytes in the base of the epidermis constantly divide and move upward to replace worn-away skin flakes. On their way, they carry melanin toward the skin's surface, and this is what produces a suntan.

DATA SEARCH

- Skin colour results from a mix of melanin, carotene (a yellow-orange pigment), and the pinkness of blood.

- Everyone has about the same number of melanocytes. However, the melanocytes in people with dark skin produce more melanin than those in people with lighter skin.

- Even in small amounts, sunlight stimulates the production of vitamin D in the skin. This vitamin is needed to absorb the mineral calcium from food that is being digested in the small intestine. Calcium is essential for healthy bones and teeth.

- In some people melanin accumulates in patches of skin. These patches are called freckles.

PATHOGENS AND PARASITES

Day to day, our bodies can come under attack from pathogens (disease-causing invaders) and parasites (organisms living in or on another species and actually existing at its expense).

The definitions overlap because pathogens are parasites, and parasites cause disease. Pathogen refers to microorganisms such as viruses (nonliving infective chemical packages), bacteria (simple cells, some of which cause disease by releasing toxins), and protists (larger single cells, mostly harmless), while parasite usually describes something bigger, such as parasitic fungi or tapeworms.

BACTERIA ARE THE SMALLEST AND MOST ABUNDANT OF LIVING THINGS ON THE PLANET— MOST ARE HARMLESS OR EVEN BENEFICIAL TO US.

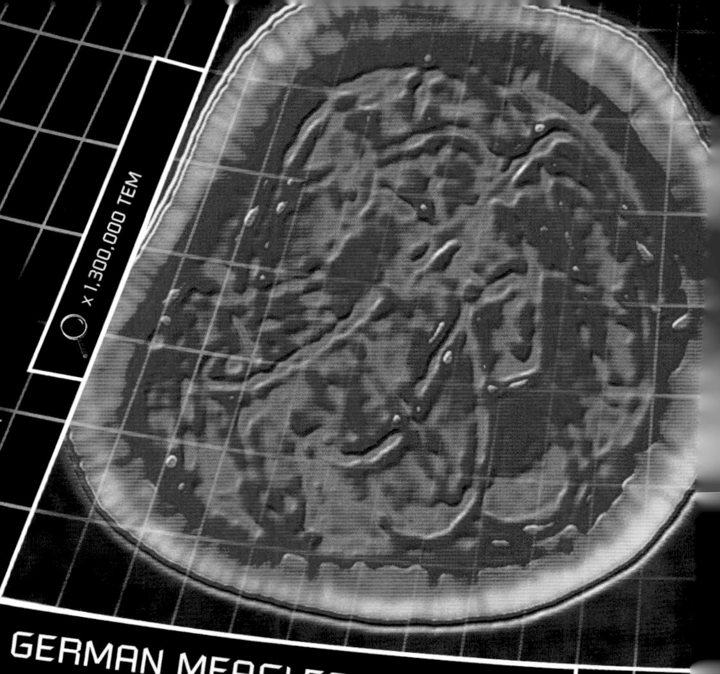

x 1,300,000 TEM

GERMAN MEASLES

This section through a rubella (German measles) virus shows the basic structure common to all viruses. An outer protective protein coat (yellow) surrounds strands of genetic material (red/purple) that carry the instructions to make more viruses. Spread by airborne droplets, the virus usually causes a mild rash, but in pregnant women it can damage the fetus. Thanks to routine childhood vaccinations, rubella is no longer a common disease.

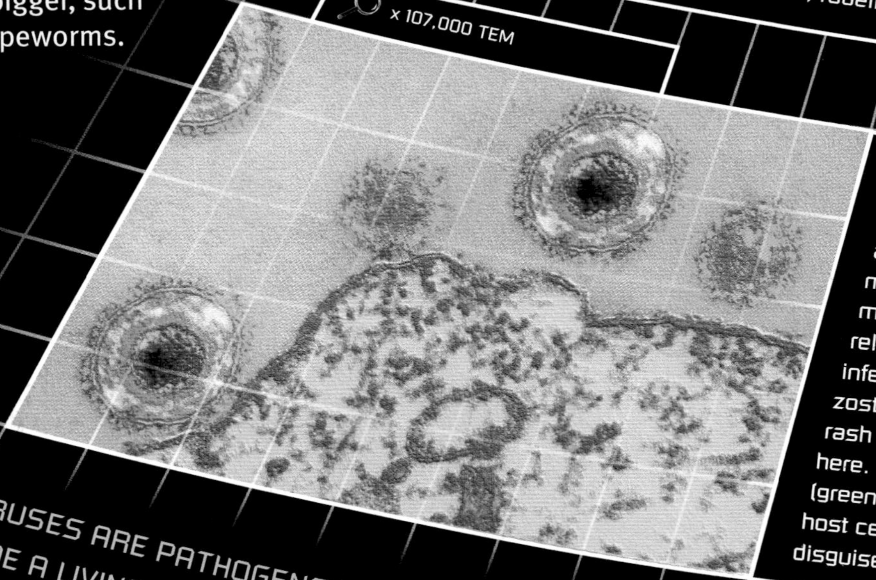

x 107,000 TEM

CHICKEN POX

To reproduce, a virus must invade a living cell. Once inside, its genetic material hijacks the cell to make multiple copies of itself. These are released from the host cell ready to infect others. Newly made varicella zoster viruses that cause the itchy rash known as chicken pox are shown here. They have an outer envelope (green) acquired from part of their host cell (bottom right) that helps to disguise them from the body's defenses.

ALL VIRUSES ARE PATHOGENS BECAUSE THEY HAVE TO INVADE A LIVING BACTERIAL, PLANT, OR ANIMAL CELL IN ORDER TO REPRODUCE THEMSELVES.

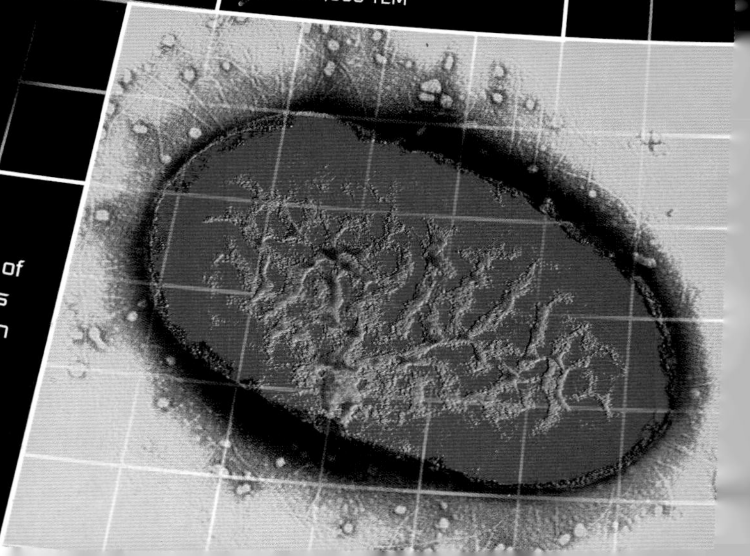

x 51,000 TEM

WHOOPING COUGH

Bordatella pertussis, shown here in section, is one of the bacteria that are pathogenic in humans. It causes whooping cough, or pertussis, a disease spread when infected droplets are breathed in. The rod-shaped bacterium uses hairlike pili (around the bacterium) to attach to respiratory cells. It then releases toxins that cause the characteristic cough and "whoop." Although this can be a dangerous disease in children, its occurrence has been reduced by vaccination.

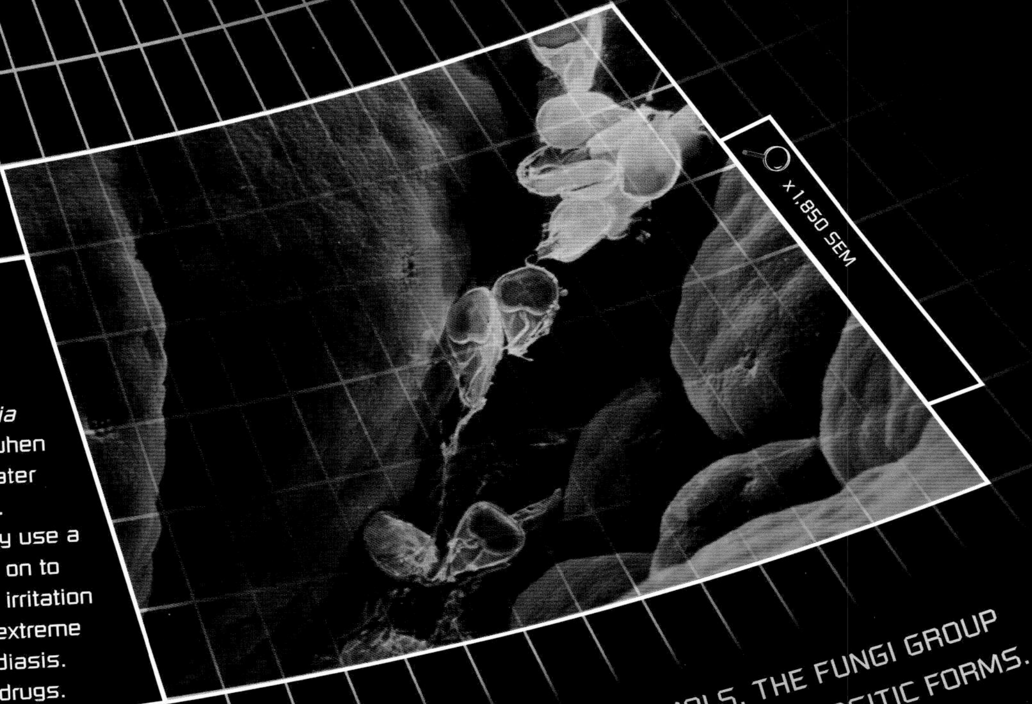

x 1,850 SEM

GIARDIASIS

Wandering among the villi of the small intestines (red) are these pear-shaped protists called *giardia lamblia*. They get into the body when someone eats food or drinks water contaminated by infected feces. Once in the small intestines, they use a sucking disk (dark green) to grip on to the intestinal wall. The resulting irritation causes abdominal cramps and extreme diarrhea, a condition called giardiasis. The disease can be cured with drugs.

FUNGI ARE NEITHER PLANTS NOR ANIMALS. THE FUNGI GROUP INCLUDES MUSHROOMS, BREAD MOLDS, AND PARASITIC FORMS.

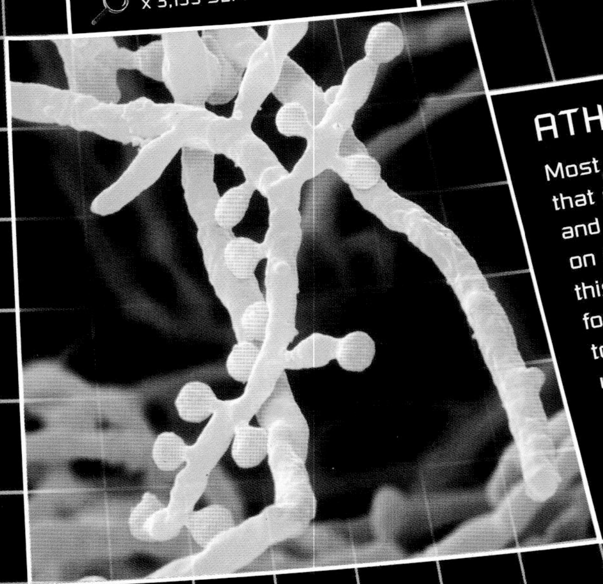

x 3,135 SEM

ATHLETE'S FOOT

Most fungi consist of hypha—long threads that grow through a food source, digesting and absorbing nutrients as they go. Many live on dead, rotting material. But some, such as this *trichophyton mentagrophytes*, prefer living food. It causes the itchy, sore skin between the toes known as athlete's foot. Thriving in damp, warm conditions, its parasitic hypha (green) feed on skin cells. Fruiting bodies (orange) release spores that spread the disease. Relief can be found through better foot hygiene and antifungal creams and powders.

A TAPEWORM CAN PRODUCE A MILLION EGGS EVERY DAY AND LIVE FOR MORE THAN 20 YEARS.

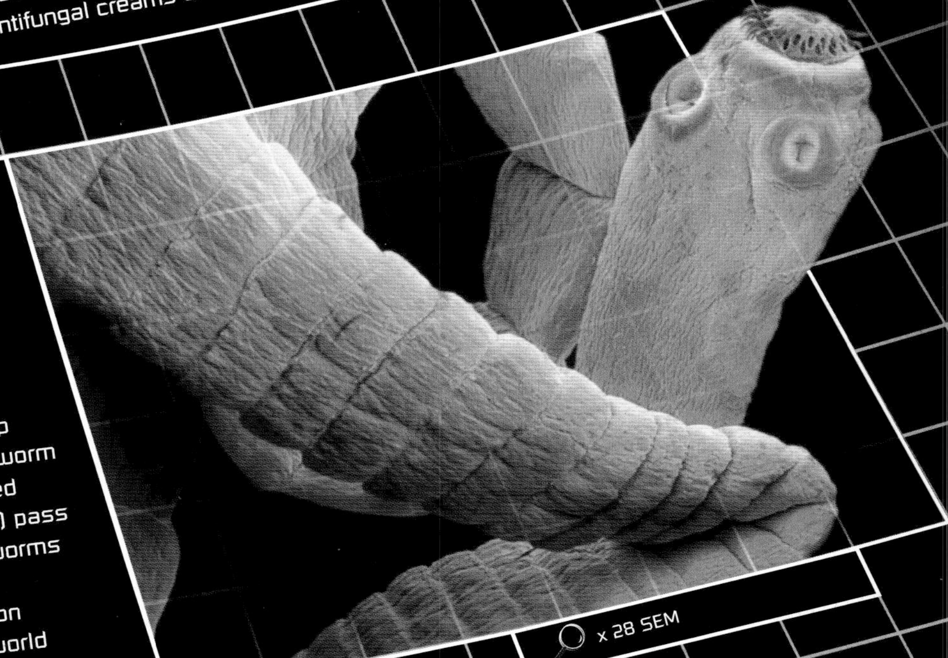

TAPEWORM

This long, ribbonlike parasite lives in the intestines, wallowing in and absorbing part-digested food. At 16 ft (5 m) or more in length, it is difficult to show a whole tapeworm. What can be seen here is the scolex (head region), which has suckers and hooks that grip the intestinal wall to prevent the tapeworm from being swept away. When packed with eggs, the proglottids (segments) pass out with the feces. People get tapeworms by eating pork or beef infected with tapeworm larvae. Tapeworm infection is less common in the developed world because of improved public health.

x 28 SEM

INSECT INVADER

By accident, a mosquito has flown inside the ear. It can be felt moving around, and its incredibly loud buzzing threatens to cause all-out panic. However, the body's natural defenses—earwax and hairs—are on hand to prevent the insect from reaching and damaging the delicate eardrum.

EARDRUM

MOSQUITO

EARWAX

EAR CANAL

EAR HAIR

ENVIRONMENT:
Attached to the roof of the ear canal, Nanocam is just inside the ear observing the intruder.

PROTECTIVE WAX

Your ear is the sense organ that detects sounds. An opening in the outer ear flap leads to the ear canal. This carries sound waves to the eardrum, to which are attached tiny bones. These relay vibrations to sensors in the innermost part of the ear. The skin-lined ear canal is cleaned by earwax (cerumen), which also acts as a repellent to any insects trying to enter.

FIRST RESPONSES

- Touch sensors in the skin lining the ear canal detect the mosquito's presence and send messages to the brain.

- Sound of buzzing, detected by the ear, creates feeling of discomfort.

- Head tilted to one side and shaken in an attempt to dislodge the insect.

1 »

Female mosquito
Insect that pierces skin to feed on human blood.

Ear canal
1 in- (2.5 cm-) long passage, from the outside to the eardrum.

INFILTRATED EAR

In search of a possible blood meal, a female mosquito has landed on the pinna—the outer flap of the ear, close to the entrance of the ear canal. Although most insects would not travel any farther into the ear, this mosquito has unintentionally found its way into the dark, tunnel-like ear canal. Immediately, this sensitive part of the body is under threat.

2 »

Earwax
Secretion that lubricates and cleans the ear canal.

STICKY TRAP IS SET

Glands in the skin of the outer part of the ear canal produce waxy cerumen. This combines with oily sebum, sweat, and skin flakes to form sticky earwax. Once the mosquito starts to move along the ear canal, the unwelcome visitor finds herself trapped by the gluey earwax. With her feet stuck, the mosquito struggles to move in any direction.

3 »

Ear canal hairs
Grow from hair follicles in the skin of the ear canal.

MOVEMENT HAMPERED

In addition to producing earwax, the skin in the outer part of the ear also has short hairs. These hairs get tangled up with the mosquito's long legs, creating another serious obstacle to any further progress through the ear. The body's defenses have combined successfully to stop the struggling insect in its tracks.

4 »

Eardrum
Taut membrane that separates the ear canal from the middle ear.

BUZZ REACHES BRAIN

The insect beats its wings in an attempt to escape, producing high speed vibrations, or sound waves, that cause the eardrum to vibrate. These vibrations get relayed to the inner ear, which sends messages to the brain so a loud buzzing is heard. The brain responds and the head is shaken vigorously. The mosquito exits in a frenzy of beating wings.

DATA SEARCH

- Digging inside the ear with a finger, cotton swab, or other object to try and dislodge an insect is dangerous. The insect gets pushed in farther and could damage the eardrum.

- Earwax can be a variety of colors, including yellow, orange, gray, and brown. It can be either moist or dry.

- Every day, new wax pushes old wax toward the ear's opening. Although they are too tiny to see, clumps of old wax fall out whenever you talk, yawn, or chew.

- Earwigs get their name from an ancient belief that they are able to crawl into a sleeping person's ear and burrow into the brain. Fortunately, this is not true, so you can sleep easier at night!

FIGHT OR FLIGHT

When you feel threatened, the body has a fast-acting mechanism to deal with the danger. The brain sets off a rapid response by triggering the release of the hormone adrenalin. This prepares the body for flight or fight—running away or confronting the threat.

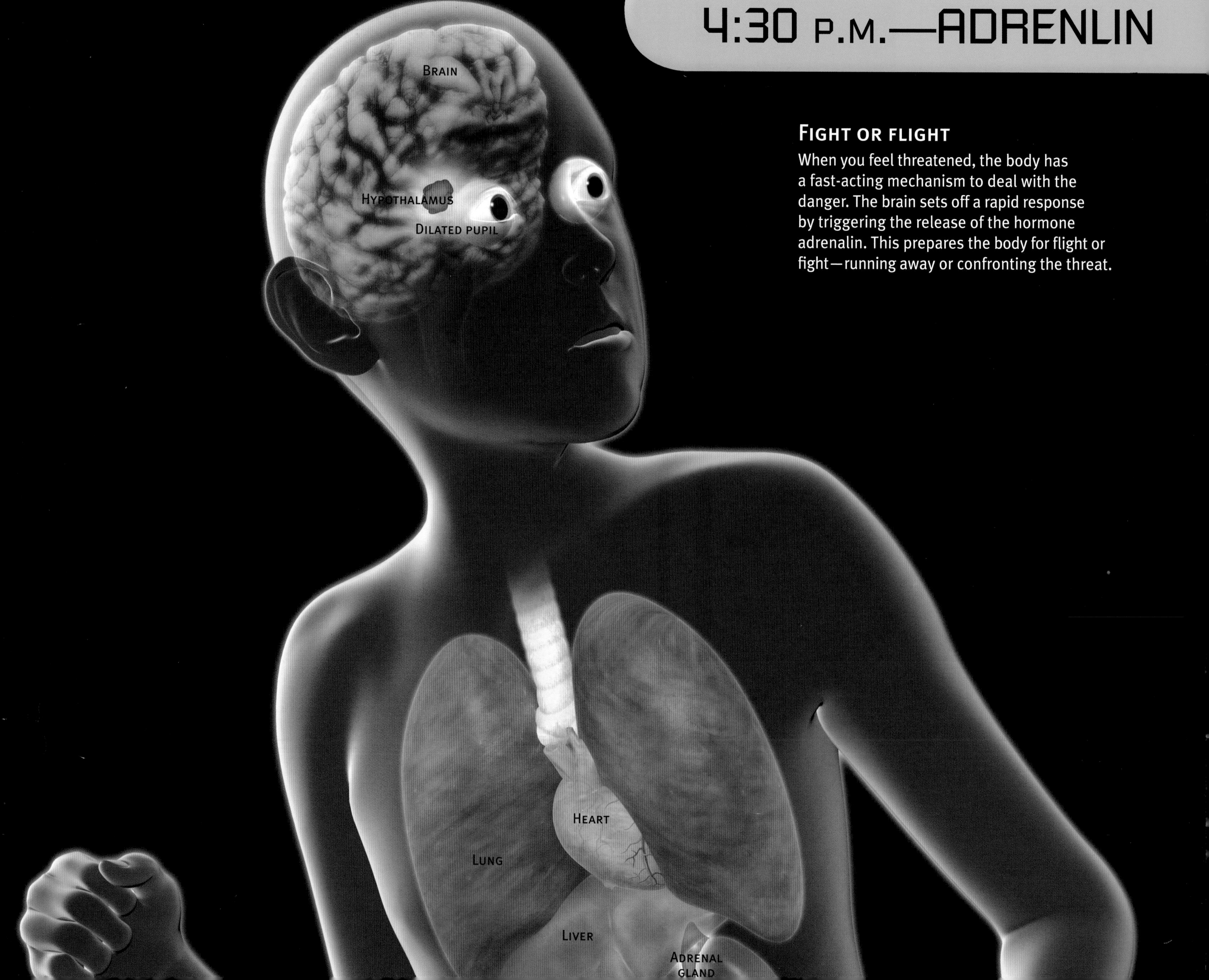

BRAIN

HYPOTHALAMUS

DILATED PUPIL

HEART

LUNG

LIVER

ADRENAL GLAND

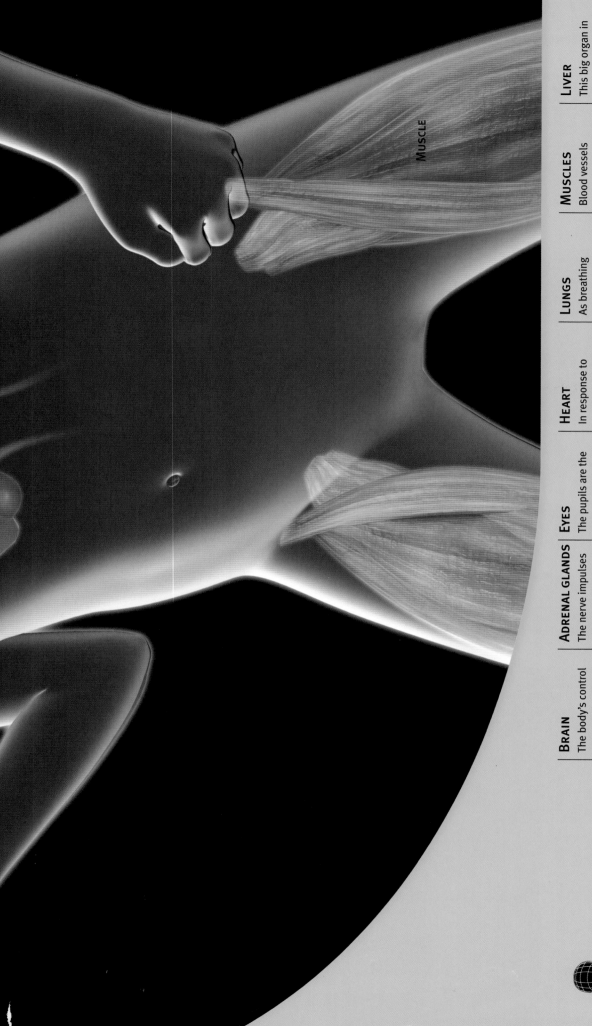

MUSCLE

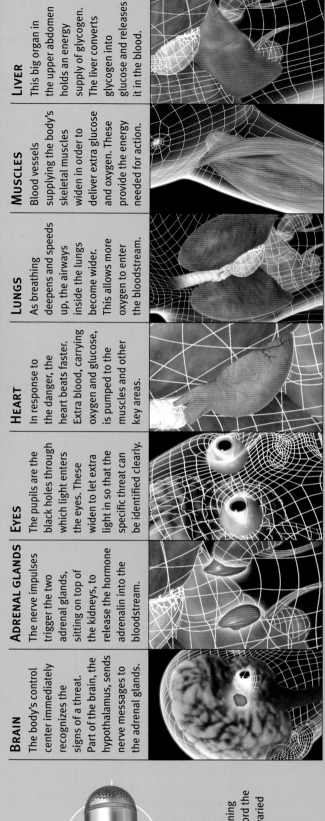

BRAIN

The body's control center immediately recognizes the signs of a threat. Part of the brain, the hypothalamus, sends nerve messages to the adrenal glands.

ADRENAL GLANDS

The nerve impulses trigger the two adrenal glands, sitting on top of the kidneys, to release the hormone adrenalin into the bloodstream.

EYES

The pupils are the black holes through which light enters the eyes. These widen to let extra light in so that the specific threat can be identified clearly.

HEART

In response to the danger, the heart beats faster. Extra blood, carrying oxygen and glucose, is pumped to the muscles and other key areas.

LUNGS

As breathing deepens and speeds up, the airways inside the lungs become wider. This allows more oxygen to enter the bloodstream.

MUSCLES

Blood vessels supplying the body's skeletal muscles widen in order to deliver extra glucose and oxygen. These provide the energy needed for action.

LIVER

This big organ in the upper abdomen holds an energy supply of glycogen. The liver converts glycogen into glucose and releases it in the blood.

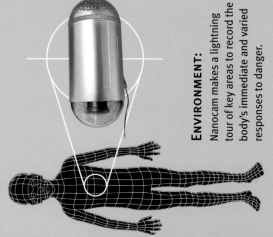

ENVIRONMENT:

Nanocam makes a lightning tour of key areas to record the body's immediate and varied responses to danger.

DEFENSE SYSTEMS

When threatened, the body rapidly alters its internal workings to become stronger, faster, and more alert. The key to this is the heart. Stimulated by adrenalin and the nervous system, it beats faster, increasing the supply of oxygen to the muscles and brain, so the body can confront the threat or escape.

× 500

AORTA
CARRIES OXYGEN-RICH BLOOD
FROM LEFT VENTRICLE
TO THE BODY

PULMONARY ARTERY
CARRIES OXYGEN-POOR BLOOD
FROM RIGHT VENTRICLE
TO THE LUNGS

LEFT ATRIUM

SEMILUNAR VALVE

SEMILUNAR VALVE

BICUSPID VALVE

SINOATRIAL NODE

RIGHT ATRIUM

TRICUSPID VALVE

HEART STRINGS

SEPTUM

LEFT VENTRICLE

RIGHT VENTRICLE

FIRST RESPONSES

- Sight, sound, or thought of a threat causes brain to send nerve messages to the adrenal glands and other organs to prepare the body for action.

- Adrenal glands release adrenalin, which, acting with the nervous system, increases heart rate, breathing, and blood flow, and releases energy-rich glucose.

- Blood flow to digestive system and skin decreases.

DATA SEARCH

- It is not just the sight or sound of imminent danger that triggers the "fight or flight" response. It could be something much less serious, such as the thought of taking a test or having to visit the dentist.

- The heart beats around 100,800 times every day, which is nearly 2.7 billion times in an average lifetime, without ever taking a rest.

- The body's volume of blood is over 1 gallon (5 liters) and the heart pumps this around the body every minute. About 4,000 gallons (15,000 liters) of blood pass through the heart daily—enough to fill 100 bathtubs.

- A "normal" rate for a heartbeat is about 70 beats per minute. But if someone is feeling extremely scared, their heart rate can increase to 180 beats per minute.

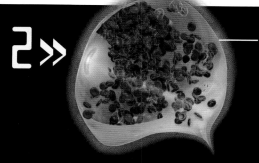

1 » *Sinoatrial node* Pacemaker that triggers and regulates heartbeat.

2 » *Atrium* One of two (left and right) upper chambers of the heart.

SETTING THE PACE

Located in the wall of the heart's right atrium, the sinoatrial node, or pacemaker, sets the heart rate. It sends out regular pulses of electrical impulses that spread through the heart's muscular wall. Adrenalin released into the bloodstream, together with nerve messages from the brain, cause the pacemaker to "fire" more rapidly.

UPPER CHAMBERS AT WORK

Blood arrives in the right atrium from the body (oxygen-poor blood) and in the left atrium from the lungs (oxygen-rich blood). Electrical impulses from the pacemaker pass through the walls of the two atria and trigger the contraction of cardiac (heart) muscle. The atria contract together, squeezing blood into the ventricles below.

3 » *Ventricle* One of two (left and right) lower chambers of the heart.

4 » *Valve* Prevents the backflow of blood from ventricle into the atrium.

VENTRICLES INCREASE FLOW

Just after the atria contract, the pacemaker's message arrives in the ventricles. In this state of emergency, the activated pacemaker makes the ventricles contract more rapidly than normal. The left ventricle greatly increases the flow of oxygen-rich blood to the muscles, while the right ventricle pumps out extra blood to the lungs.

VALVES SLAM SHUT

However fast the heart is beating, valves make sure the flow of blood is one way. This valve stops blood from flowing backward when the ventricle contracts. Other valves prevent blood from returning into the ventricles from the pulmonary artery and aorta. As valves slam shut they produce the heart sounds that can be heard using a stethoscope.

ADRENALIN

This micrograph (x 11) shows crystals of the hormone adrenalin. It is always present in the blood in small amounts but, when the body is threatened, large amounts of adrenalin are secreted into the blood from the adrenal glands. This happens in response to messages from the sympathetic nervous system, the part of the nervous system that prepares the body for action. In emergencies, adrenalin is used by doctors to restart a stopped heart and to relieve life-threatening reactions to insect stings.

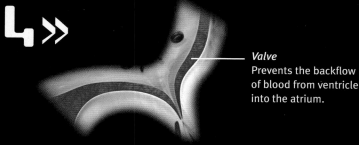

TRACHEA

ALLERGENS

RIB

RIGHT LUNG

PLEURAL MEMBRANE

BRONCHUS

INTERCOSTAL MUSCLE

DIAPHRAGM

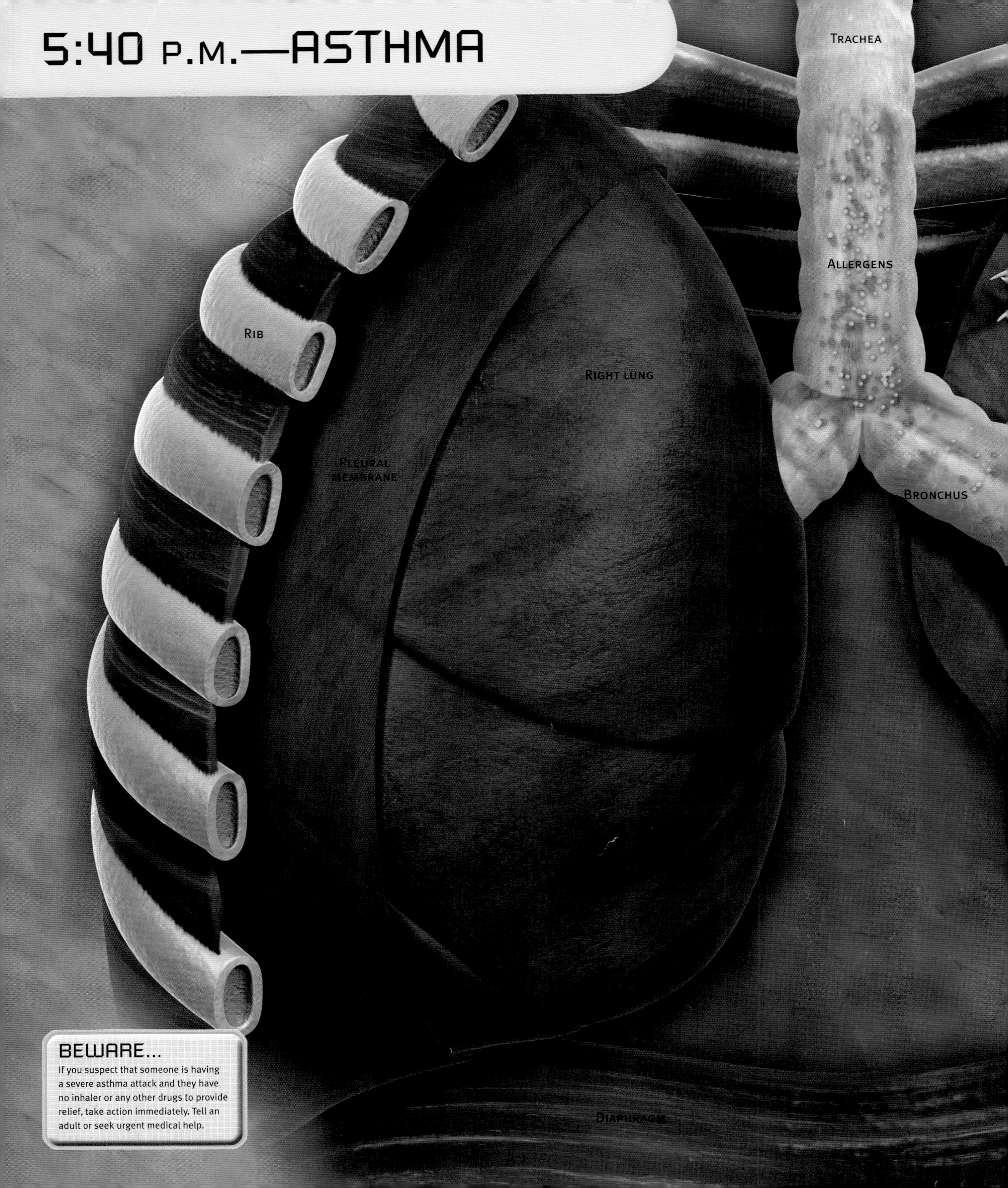

BEWARE...
If you suspect that someone is having a severe asthma attack and they have no inhaler or any other drugs to provide relief, take action immediately. Tell an adult or seek urgent medical help.

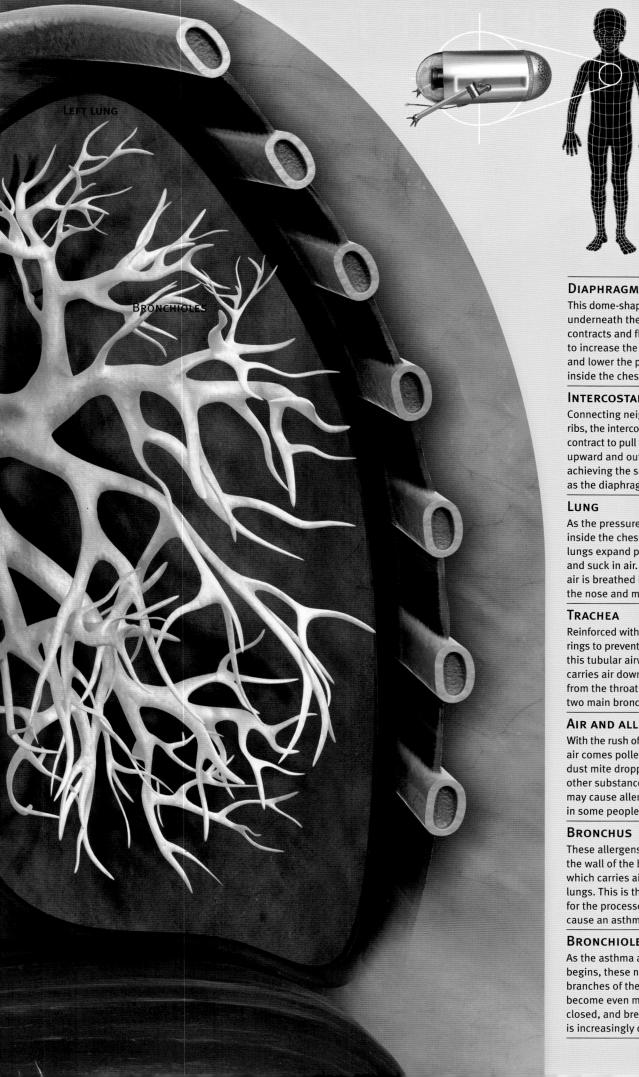

LEFT LUNG

BRONCHIOLES

NARROW AIRWAYS

Every breath we take brings with it a range of particles large and small. These particles cause an allergic response in some people. The result is an asthma attack, which narrows the air passages in the lungs, causing shortness of breath and wheezing.

ENVIRONMENT:
Hanging on with its grappling hook, and with its emergency indicator lit, Nanocam watches events in the lungs.

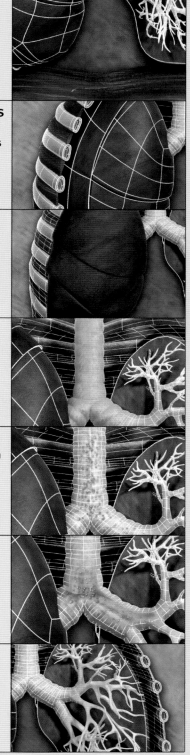

DIAPHRAGM
This dome-shaped muscle underneath the lungs contracts and flattens to increase the space and lower the pressure inside the chest.

INTERCOSTAL MUSCLES
Connecting neighboring ribs, the intercostal muscles contract to pull the rib cage upward and outward, achieving the same effect as the diaphragm.

LUNG
As the pressure decreases inside the chest cavity, the lungs expand passively and suck in air. As a result, air is breathed in through the nose and mouth.

TRACHEA
Reinforced with cartilage rings to prevent collapse, this tubular airway carries air downward from the throat into the two main bronchi.

AIR AND ALLERGENS
With the rush of breathed-in air comes pollen grains, dust mite droppings, and other substances that may cause allergies in some people.

BRONCHUS
These allergens settle on the wall of the bronchus, which carries air into the lungs. This is the trigger for the processes that cause an asthma attack.

BRONCHIOLES
As the asthma attack begins, these narrow branches of the bronchi become even more closed, and breathing is increasingly difficult.

DEFENSE SYSTEMS

During an asthma attack, the body's defenses overreact to substances (allergens) that are normally harmless. This causes the airways—bronchi and bronchioles—inside the lungs to become inflamed, narrow, and partly blocked with mucus. Air flow is restricted, making breathing difficult and causing wheezing.

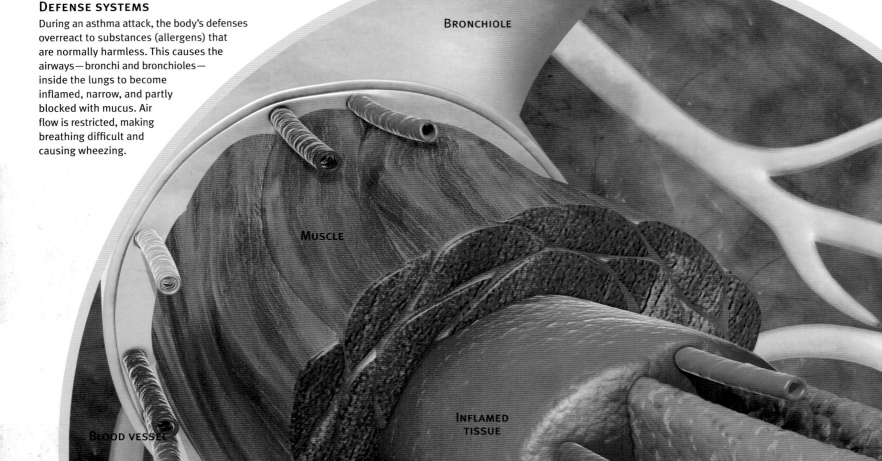

BRONCHIOLE

MUSCLE

BLOOD VESSEL

INFLAMED TISSUE

EPITHELIUM

LUMEN

FIRST RESPONSES

- Allergens (substances that trigger allergies) in breathed-in air are detected by body's immune (defense) system.

- Immune system releases antibodies to target allergens.

- Antibodies bind to allergens, but this also causes release of the chemical histamine, which triggers an asthma attack.

- Adrenal glands release adrenalin—this helps to open the airway and limit the attack.

DATA SEARCH

- Allergens floating in the air that trigger asthma attacks can include pollen, mold spores, and dust mite droppings, as well as skin flakes or fur from household pets such as cats and dogs.

- Asthma that starts in adulthood is not usually triggered solely by allergens. It could be exercise, cold air, smoke, pollution, or stress that sets off attacks.

- People who have asthma often use inhalers to control their breathing. The inhaler delivers a measured dose of a drug directly into the airways. For quick relief, a bronchodilator (reliever) relaxes smooth muscle and makes the bronchi and bronchioles wide. For longer-term prevention, a corticosteroid (preventer) is used to reduce mucus production and inflammation.

1 »

Inflammation
The body's response to foreign substances is increased blood flow to affected area.

2 »

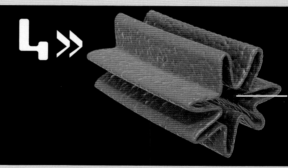

Epithelium
Bronchiole lining includes cells that produce the thick slippery fluid called mucus.

INFLAMED LINING

A look inside a bronchiole reveals what is happening during an asthma attack. When allergens trigger the release of histamine, the first response is inflammation. Blood vessels get wider, increasing the blood flow to the bronchiole, and become more leaky, allowing fluid to seep into the bronchiole wall.

MORE AND MORE MUCUS

As a result of the increased blood flow, the inner part of the bronchiole becomes red and swollen. This inflammation stimulates specific cells in the bronchiole lining to increase greatly their mucus production. Mucus is normally produced in small amounts to trap any dust particles in the air.

3 »

Smooth muscle
Type of muscle found in the wall of airways and other body tubes.

4 »

Lumen
Hollow space in the center of bronchiole.

SQUEEZED BRONCHIOLE

Arranged spirally in the wall of the bronchiole are smooth muscle cells. Smooth muscle is involuntary. Unlike the skeletal muscles that move the body, you cannot decide to make smooth muscle contract. In this case, histamine released as part of the allergic response makes the smooth muscle contract and squeeze inward.

NARROW AIRWAY

The combination of inflammation and contraction of smooth muscle makes the lumen of the bronchiole narrower. The narrowing worsens as sticky mucus clogs up the lumen. Breathing becomes difficult as the lung's narrowed passages greatly reduce the flow of air. In time, the body releases adrenalin to open the airways, or an inhaler provides a quick fix.

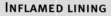

MUCUS

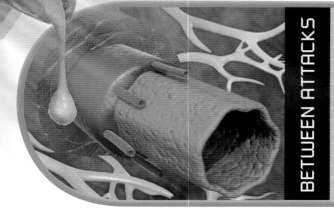

BETWEEN ATTACKS

This image shows a section through one of the lung's bronchioles as it would appear between asthma attacks or in someone who does not suffer from asthma. The muscle layer in the bronchiole wall is relaxed so that the inner lumen of the bronchiole is at its widest. The epithelium lining the bronchiole is not inflamed, nor is it covered by excessive amounts of mucus. In this healthy state, the bronchiole's wide lumen allows air to flow freely without wheezing or breathlessness.

OUTER DEFENSES

The body is under threat of attack 24/7 from a wide range of pathogenic bacteria, viruses, fungi, and other microorganisms that cause disease.

Tackling this threat is the job of the body's immune system. Its outer defenses are physical, chemical, and living barriers that stop invaders before they can get farther inside the body. Physical barriers include the skin and membranes that line cavities such as the mouth and trachea. Chemical warfare is waged through saliva, tears, mucus, and gastric juice. Living barriers include the

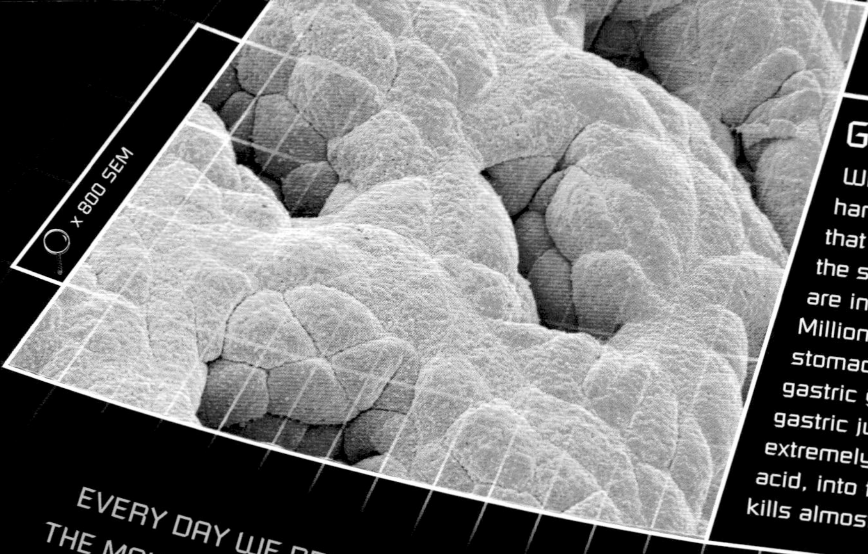

x 800 SEM

GASTRIC JUICE

Whether harmful or harmless, any bacteria that piggyback their way into the stomach on food and drink are in for a nasty surprise. Millions of gastric pits in the stomach lining lead to deep gastric glands. These release gastric juice, which contains extremely strong hydrochloric acid, into the stomach. The acid kills almost all invading bacteria.

EVERY DAY WE RELEASE AROUND 1 LITRE (0.2 GALLONS) OF SALIVA INTO THE MOUTH AND 2 LITRES (0.4 GALLONS) OF GASTRIC JUICE INTO THE STOMACH.

SALIVA

Also known as spit, this multipurpose fluid is squirted into the mouth from three pairs of salivary glands. This section through a gland shows an acinus—a cluster of saliva-producing cells surrounding a central duct (tube) that empties into the mouth. Saliva naturally cleans the mouth and contains the chemical lysozyme, which kills bacteria. Being alkaline, it neutralizes the acids released by tooth bacteria. Salivary mucus also moistens food for easy swallowing.

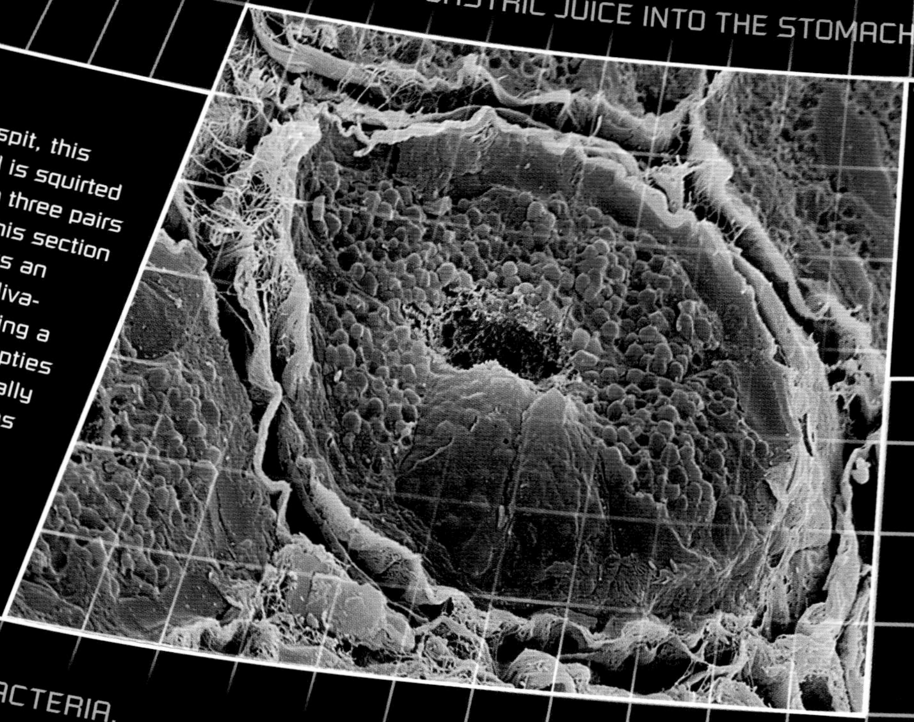

x 1,625 SEM

FECES CAN CONSIST OF UP TO 50 PERCENT BACTERIA, HENCE THE NEED TO WASH HANDS AFTER GOING TO THE BATHROOM.

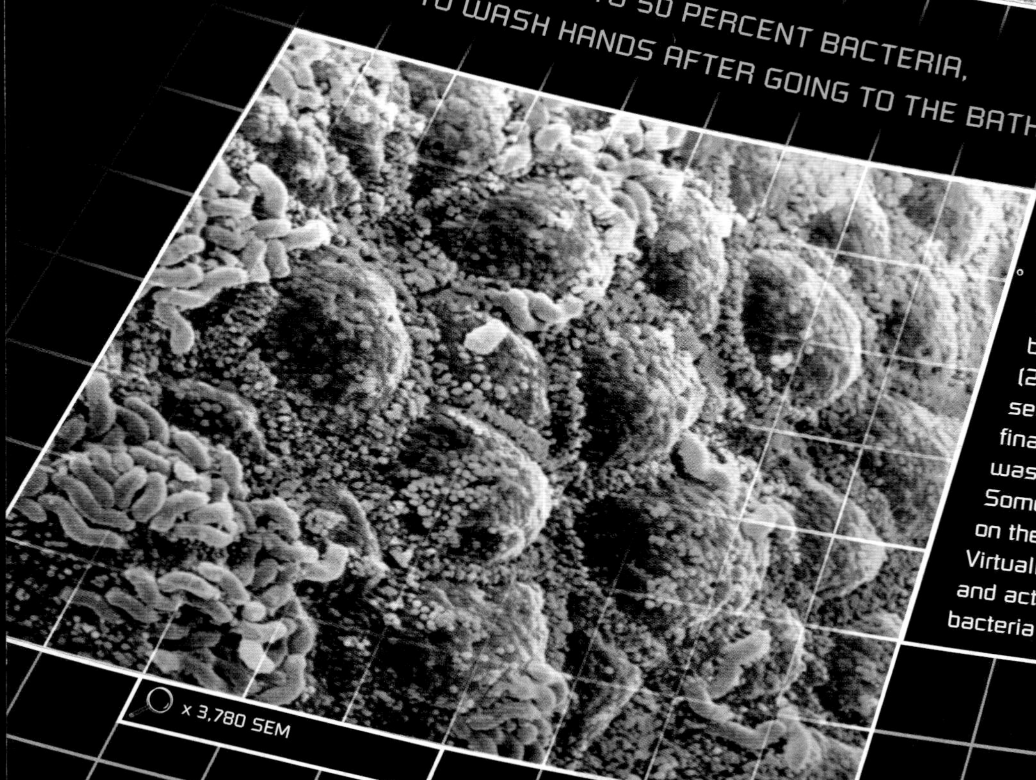

COLON BACTERIA

The digestive system contains about 100 trillion (100,000,000,000,000) bacteria weighing approximately 4 lb (2 kg). Most live in the colon, the main section of the large intestines and the final stretch of the alimentary canal, where waste is processed and exits the body. Some of these bacteria (mauve) can be seen on the lining of the colon (brown and purple). Virtually all colon bacteria are harmless, and actually benefit us by preventing harmful bacteria from entering and causing disease.

x 3,780 SEM

x 360 SEM

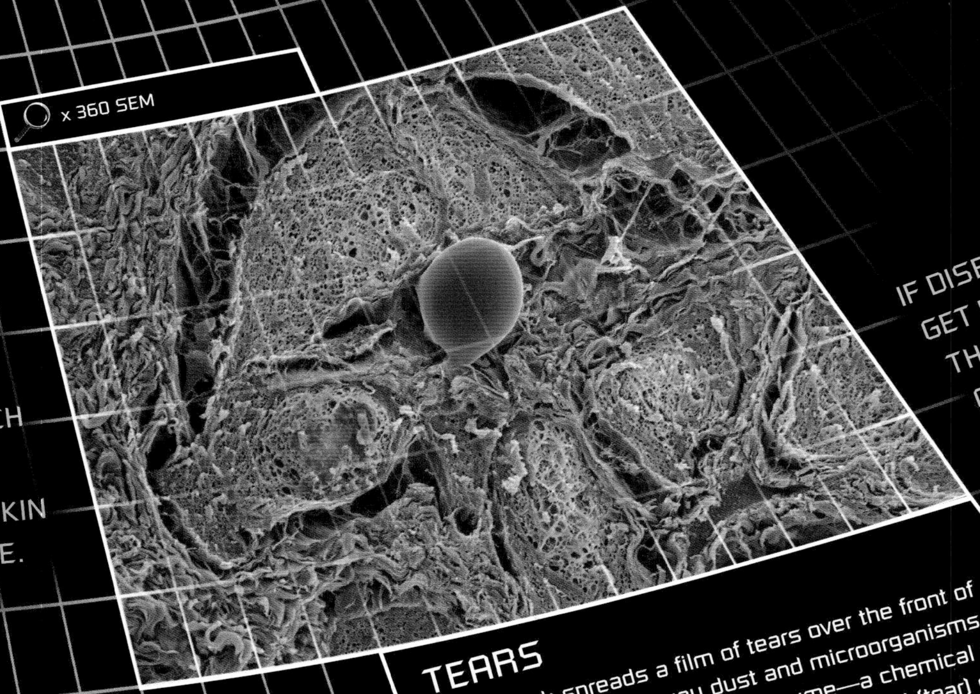

WE LOSE ABOUT
50,000 SKIN FLAKES
EVERY MINUTE, WHICH
WORKS OUT TO A
SUITCASE-FULL OF SKIN
FLAKES IN A LIFETIME.

IF DISEASE-CAUSING PATHOGENS
GET PAST THE OUTER BARRIERS,
THE NEXT LINE OF DEFENSE IS
GERM-EATING CELLS CALLED
NEUTROPHILS AND MACROPHAGES.

TEARS

Every blink spreads a film of tears over the front of
the eye, washing away dust and microorganisms.
Like saliva, tears contain lysozyme—a chemical that
kills bacteria. Tears are made by lacrimal (tear) glands
behind the eyelid. This section through a gland shows
a tear (red) and the cells (brown) that produce tears.

MUCUS IN THE TRACHEA TRAPS PATHOGENS, WHILE MUCUS IN THE

STOMACH PREVENTS ACID AND ENZYMES FROM DIGESTING ITS LINING.

x 1,135 SEM

MUCUS AND CILIA

The air we breathe in carries dust and pathogens
that could damage its final destination, the lungs.
The trachea (windpipe) has a key protective role.
The trachea's lining, shown here, removes harmful
particles and pathogens from the air in two ways.
Goblet cells (brown) produce sticky mucus, which
traps the particles. Cilia (pink) beat together to move
dirty mucus up in the throat, where it is swallowed
and then doused in acid in the stomach.

x 1,230 SEM

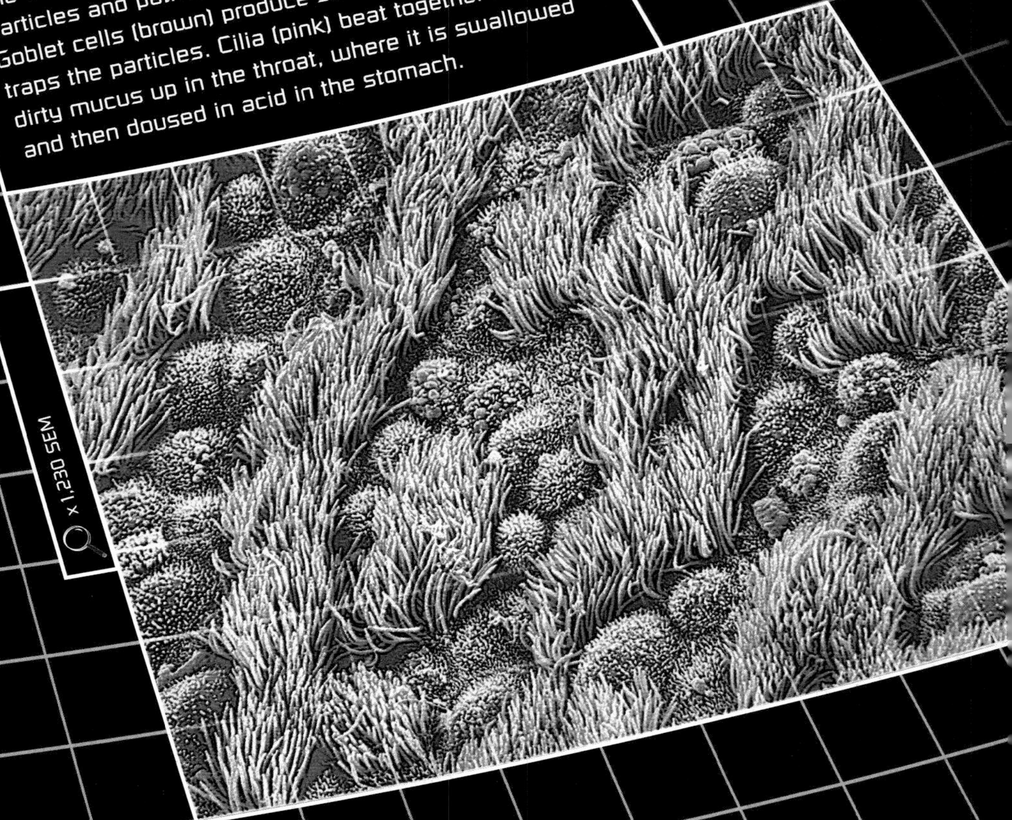

SKIN

This surface view of the skin shows
overlapping, flattened dead cells that
extend downward in the epidermis
through 20 or 30 layers. These cells are
packed with the tough protein keratin that
makes them waterproof, protects deeper
living cells against abrasions, and provides
a formidable barrier against invasion
by bacteria, fungi, or other pathogens.
These surface cells, with their pathogen
passengers, are constantly shed as skin
flakes and then replaced with cells from
the dividing layer in the deepest part of
the epidermis.

6:00 P.M.—CHOKING

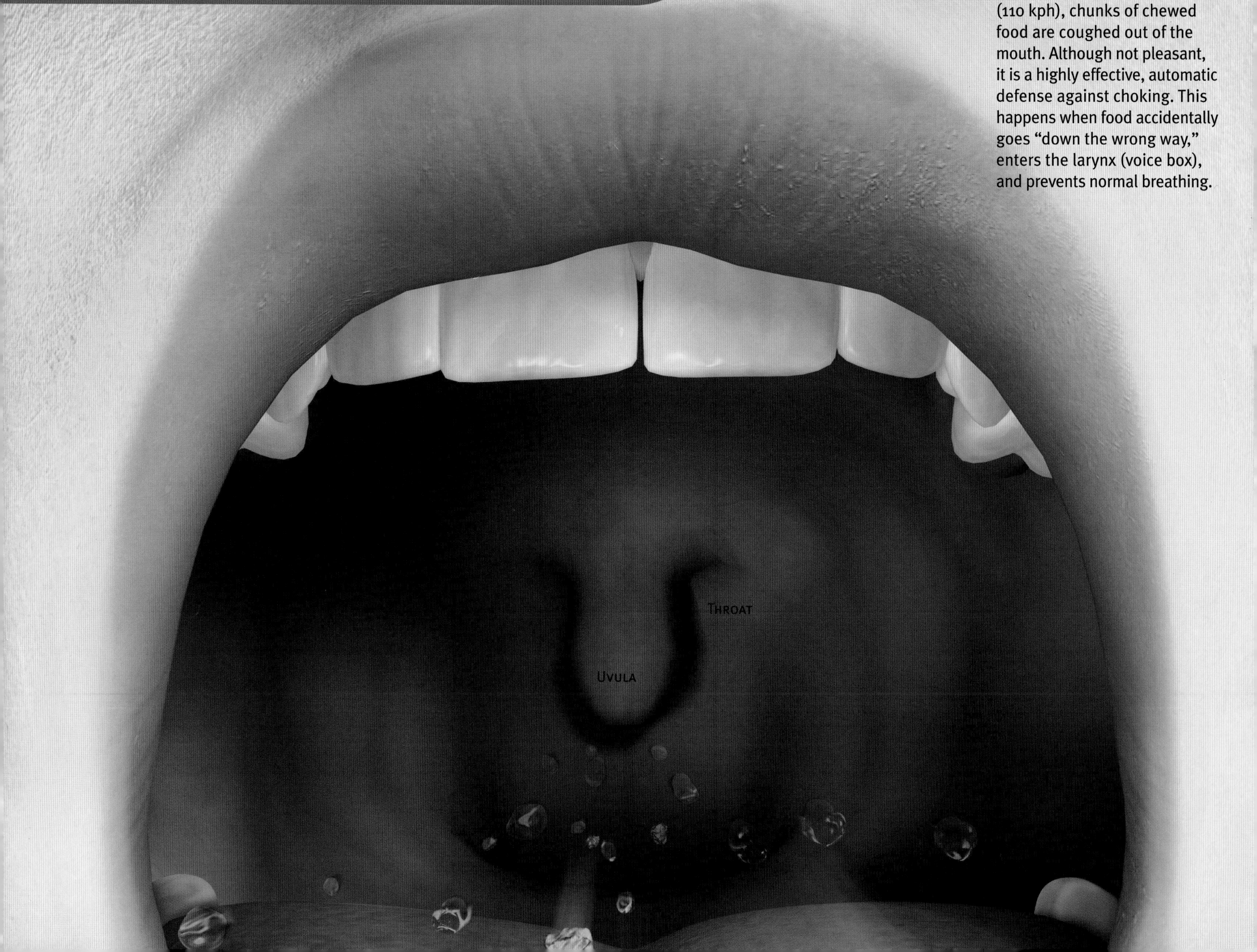

TOP SPEED

At speeds of up to 70 mph (110 kph), chunks of chewed food are coughed out of the mouth. Although not pleasant, it is a highly effective, automatic defense against choking. This happens when food accidentally goes "down the wrong way," enters the larynx (voice box), and prevents normal breathing.

THROAT

UVULA

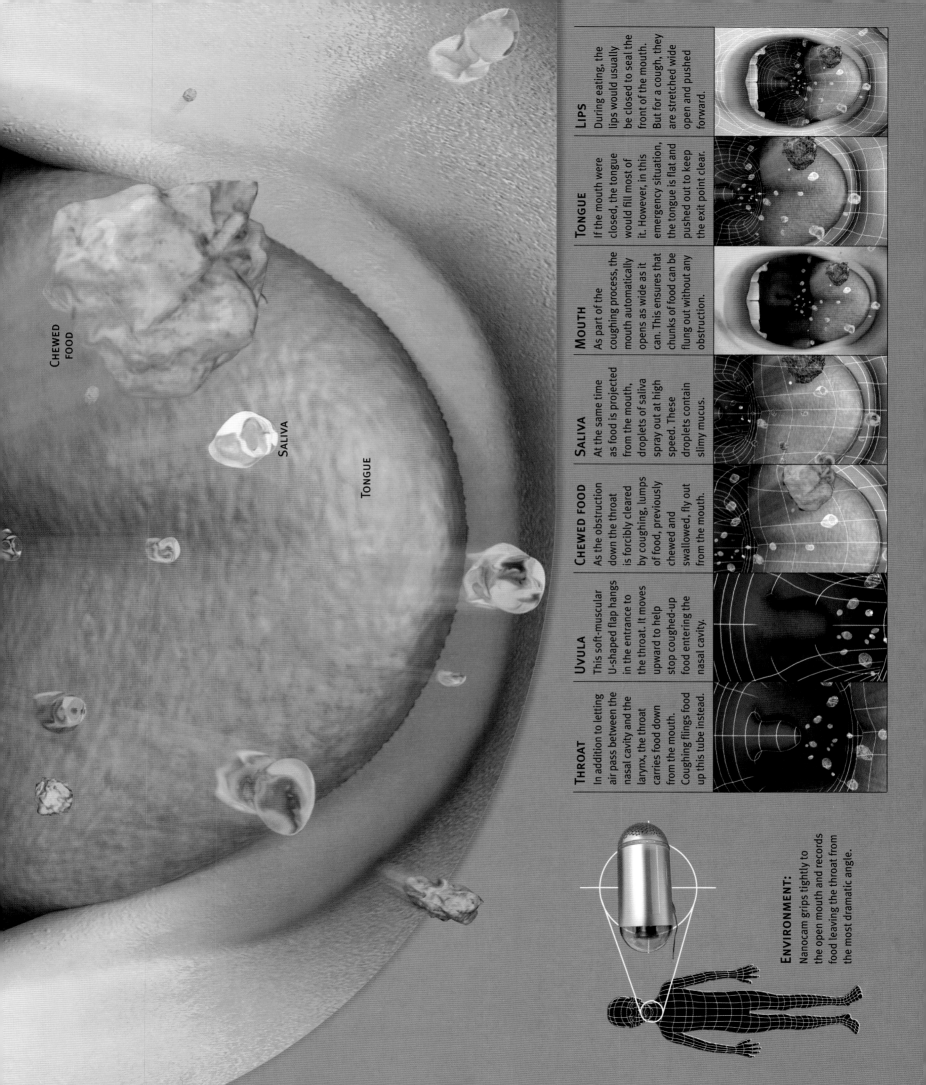

CHEWED
FOOD

SALIVA

TONGUE

THROAT

In addition to letting air pass between the nasal cavity and the larynx, the throat carries food down from the mouth. Coughing flings food up this tube instead.

UVULA

This soft-muscular U-shaped flap hangs in the entrance to the throat. It moves upward to help stop coughed-up food entering the nasal cavity.

CHEWED FOOD

As the obstruction down the throat is forcibly cleared by coughing, lumps of food, previously chewed and swallowed, fly out from the mouth.

SALIVA

At the same time as food is projected from the mouth, droplets of saliva spray out at high speed. These droplets contain slimy mucus.

MOUTH

As part of the coughing process, the mouth automatically opens as wide as it can. This ensures that chunks of food can be flung out without any obstruction.

TONGUE

If the mouth were closed, the tongue would fill most of it. However, in this emergency situation, the tongue is flat and pushed out to keep the exit point clear.

LIPS

During eating, the lips would usually be closed to seal the front of the mouth. But for a cough, they are stretched wide open and pushed forward.

ENVIRONMENT:

Nanocam grips tightly to the open mouth and records food leaving the throat from the most dramatic angle.

NANOCAM REPORT: CHOKING

Defense systems

The body has a built-in protection system to stop food from interfering with breathing by entering the larynx or trachea, which are parts of the respiratory system. But on the odd occasion, the system fails and choking results. This activates an automatic emergency response during which the offending object is coughed out.

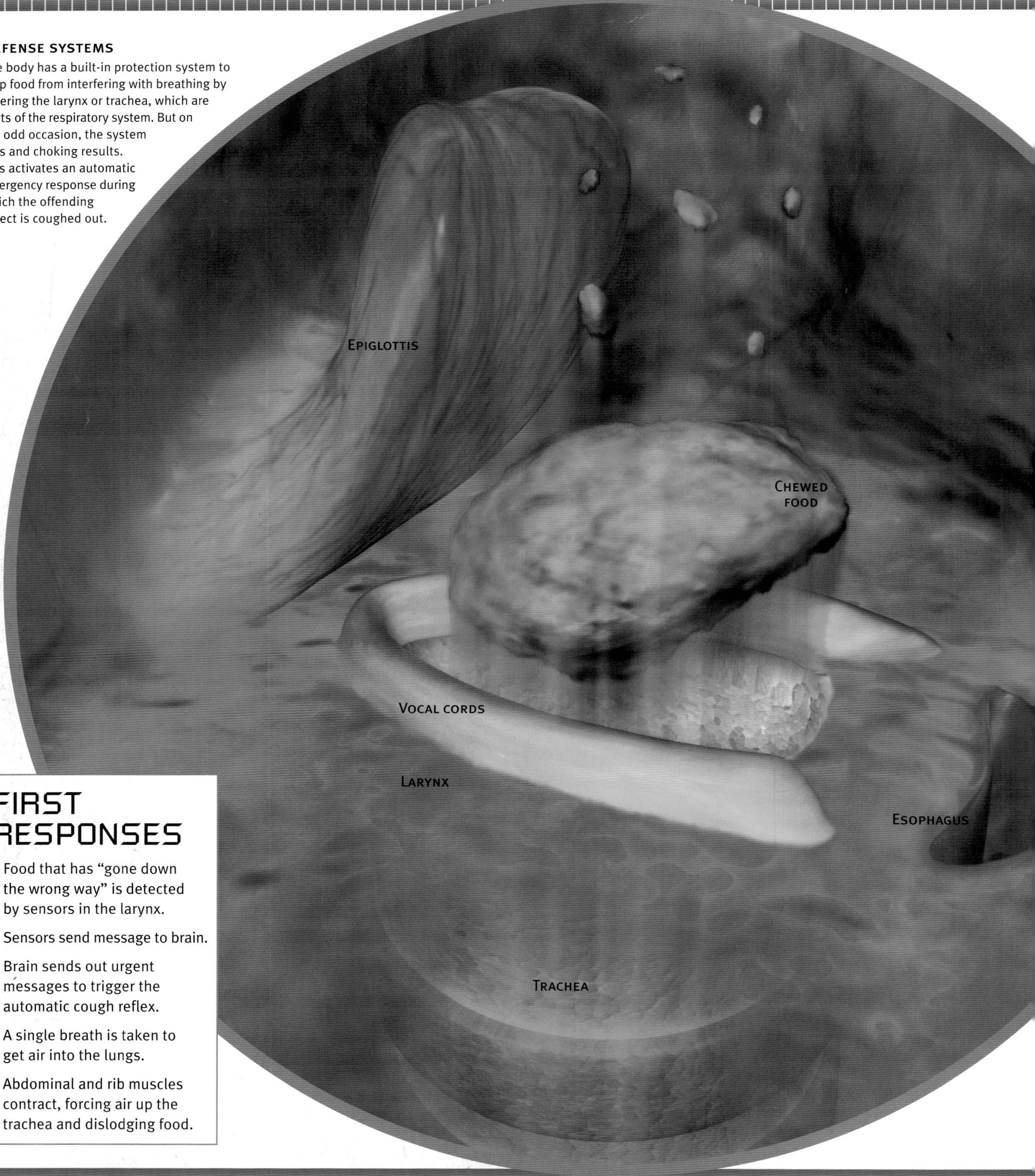

Epiglottis
Chewed food
Vocal cords
Larynx
Esophagus
Trachea

FIRST RESPONSES

- Food that has "gone down the wrong way" is detected by sensors in the larynx.
- Sensors send message to brain.
- Brain sends out urgent messages to trigger the automatic cough reflex.
- A single breath is taken to get air into the lungs.
- Abdominal and rib muscles contract, forcing air up the trachea and dislodging food.

DATA SEARCH

- There are different ways to deal with a person showing signs of choking, such as a sudden inability to talk, clutching at the throat, and hands signaling in panic. If coughing does not appear to relieve choking, they should bend over, or another person should hit them lightly between the shoulder blades. Otherwise, seek medical advice.

- The act of coughing also removes thick mucus from the trachea, which can be spat out or swallowed.

- Vocal cords in men are longer and thicker than in women and they vibrate more slowly. This makes the sound of male voices a lower pitch than female voices.

- The greater the force with which air is pushed between the vocal cords, the louder the sound that is produced.

- Singers and players of wind instruments learn to coordinate their vocal cords and pattern of breathing to create sounds of perfect pitch.

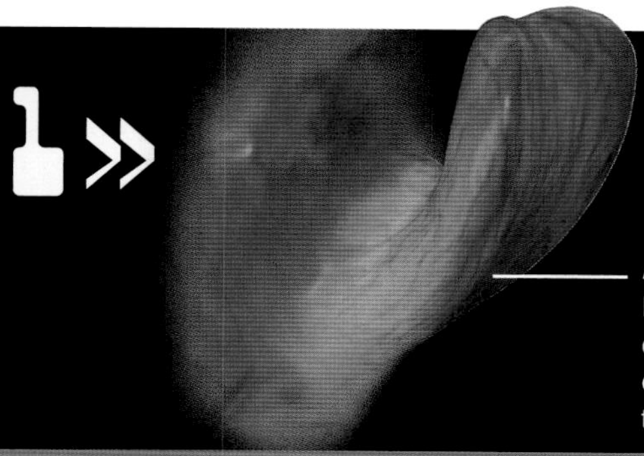

1 »

Epiglottis
Flexible flap of cartilage hinged on the front of the larynx.

2 »

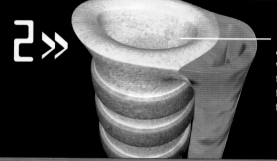

Trachea
Also called the windpipe, this is the airway leading from the larynx to the lungs.

BLOCKAGE DETECTED

Whenever food is swallowed, the epiglottis automatically tips downward to cover the entrance to the larynx. Food then enters the esophagus, the tube that carries it to the stomach. But if food slips past the epiglottis and into the larynx, the airway gets partly blocked. This causes choking and triggers the cough reflex.

PRESSURE MOUNTS

The muscles in the abdominal wall contract, as do the muscles between the ribs that pull the rib cage downward. This builds up pressure inside the chest, forcing air out of the lungs and up into the trachea. At the same time, the vocal cords in the larynx—at the top end of the trachea—shut tight.

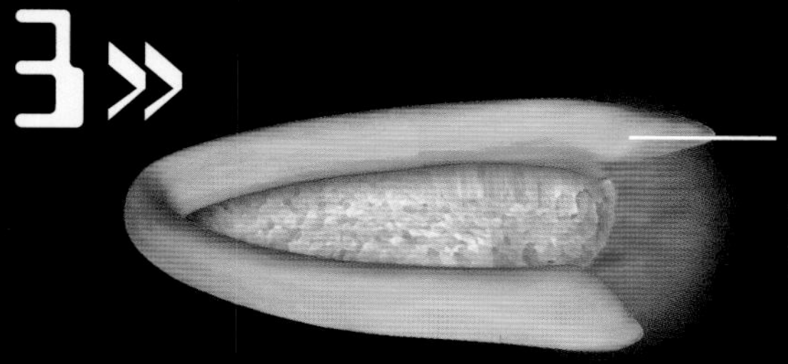

3 »

Vocal cords
Two membranes that stretch from the front to the back of the larynx.

4 »

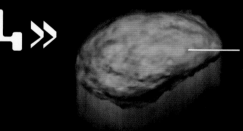

Chewed food
Soft, rounded ball consisting of pieces of food held together by mucus.

SUDDEN OPENING

Air pressure builds and builds inside the trachea. Then, in an instant, the vocal cords spring open, allowing high pressure air to rush up between them. Simultaneously, the epiglottis lifts to provide a completely clear exit up through the throat and into the mouth.

BLAST OUT

This sudden blast of air forces the lump of food quickly up the throat and out of the open mouth. The action causes the rushing sound that we know as coughing. Any smaller particles remaining in the larynx are removed by further reflex coughs.

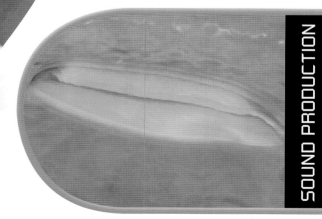

SOUND PRODUCTION

The vocal cords are the source of the sounds we make. During normal breathing, the vocal cords are open, allowing the free flow of air. For speaking, the vocal cords are drawn together, as shown here. Air expelled in controlled bursts from the lungs pushes between the vocal cords, making them vibrate and create sounds. These sounds are amplified as they pass up the throat, and get shaped into words by the tongue and lips. The brain controls this process.

6:30 P.M.—BAD TASTE

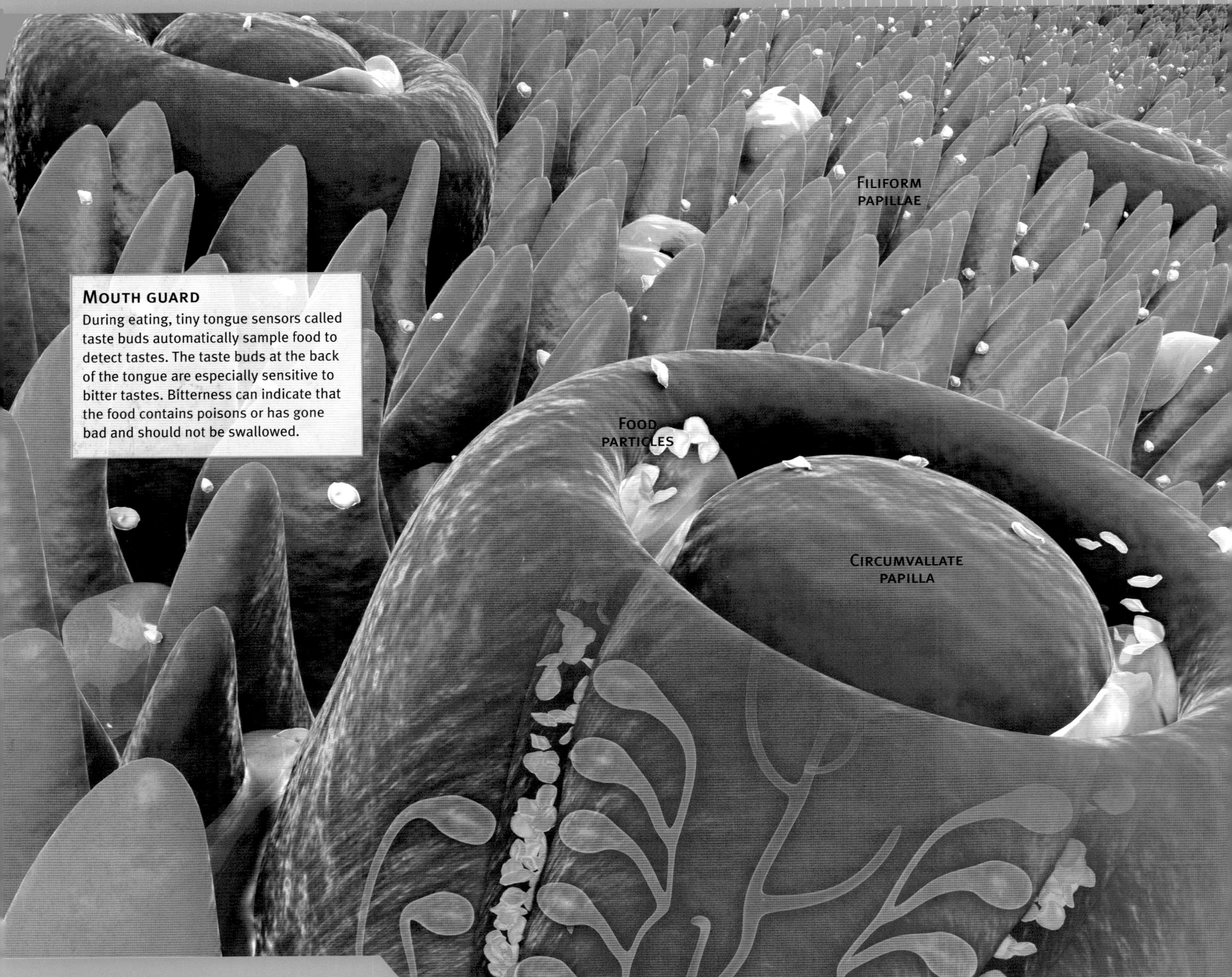

FILIFORM PAPILLAE
FOOD PARTICLES
CIRCUMVALLATE PAPILLA
TASTE BUD
SALIVA

MOUTH GUARD

During eating, tiny tongue sensors called taste buds automatically sample food to detect tastes. The taste buds at the back of the tongue are especially sensitive to bitter tastes. Bitterness can indicate that the food contains poisons or has gone bad and should not be swallowed.

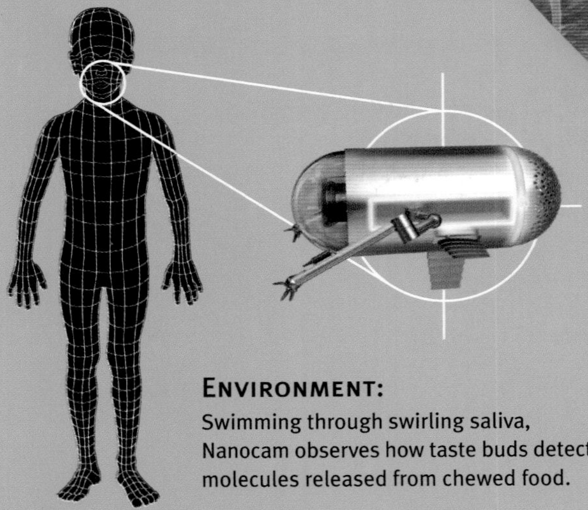

ENVIRONMENT:

Swimming through swirling saliva, Nanocam observes how taste buds detect molecules released from chewed food.

TASTE SENSATIONS

The surface of the tongue is covered with tiny bumps called papillae. Some of these papillae house taste buds that detect five basic tastes— sweet, salty, umami (meaty), sour, and bitter. While the first three tastes can make food more enjoyable, sour and bitter tastes warn us that food may be unripe, spoiled, or even poisonous.

FIRST RESPONSES

- Potentially dangerous food is chewed in the mouth.
- Taste buds detect bitter taste and send message, in the form of nerve impulses, along nerve fibers to the brain.
- Brain recognizes bitterness as a sign of bad food.
- As a precaution, brain sends instructions to spit food out.

1 »

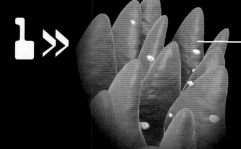

Filiform papillae
The most numerous papillae, which are arranged in parallel rows.

2 »

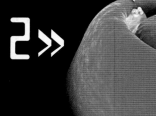

Circumvallate papilla
The larger, bitter-sensitive type of papillae.

TONGUE GRIPPERS

These spiky projections are found all over the tongue. They make the surface rough so it can grip and move food during chewing. Filiform papillae do not have taste buds. Instead, they have sensors that detect heat, cold, touch, and pain, enabling us to sense the texture and temperature of food.

BITTER AT THE BACK

Two types of papilla carry taste buds. The first are the mushroom-shaped fungiform papillae found near the front of the tongue. These detect sweet, salty, sour, and umami tastes. At the back of the tongue is a group of about 10 big circumvallate papillae. They house the taste buds sensitive to bitter tastes.

3 »

Saliva
Digestive fluid released into the mouth from six salivary glands, especially during eating.

4 »

Taste bud
Contains sensory cells that detect taste molecules.

DISSOLVING FOOD

As food is crushed by the teeth and pushed around by the tongue, watery saliva is squirted into the mouth. The tiniest particles of food dissolve in the saliva, releasing molecules that are swept over the tongue's surface. Saliva also contains slimy mucus that lubricates food so it can be swallowed easily.

DETECTING BAD TASTE

Taste molecules released from chewed food wash down the trough or "moat" inside each circumvallate papilla. Hidden in the side walls of the trough are tiers of taste pores, the openings to taste buds. Bitter taste molecules enter the pores where they are detected, and the nasty taste in the mouth is recognized.

DATA SEARCH

- There are around 10,000 taste buds on the tongue. Each taste bud contains between 30 and 100 sensory cells.

- We enjoy different foods because of their flavors. Flavor is a combination of taste, smell, texture, and temperature. Smell is the dominant component of flavor, with the nose able to detect more than 10,000 different odors.

- The durian is a tropical fruit that smells disgusting but tastes delicious. Carrying one on public transportation is usually banned!

- Our cravings for certain tastes help to ensure a balanced diet. Sweet foods provide us with energy, meaty foods contain body-building proteins, and salt is an essential part of our body fluids.

CARDIAC SPHINCTER

ESOPHAGUS

LAUNCHING LUNCH

A lunch contaminated by bacterial toxins has caused food poisoning by irritating the stomach. This initiates vomiting, a reflex (automatic) defense mechanism that will launch semidigested food and toxins out of the body through the mouth. This gets rid of the cause of the poisoning.

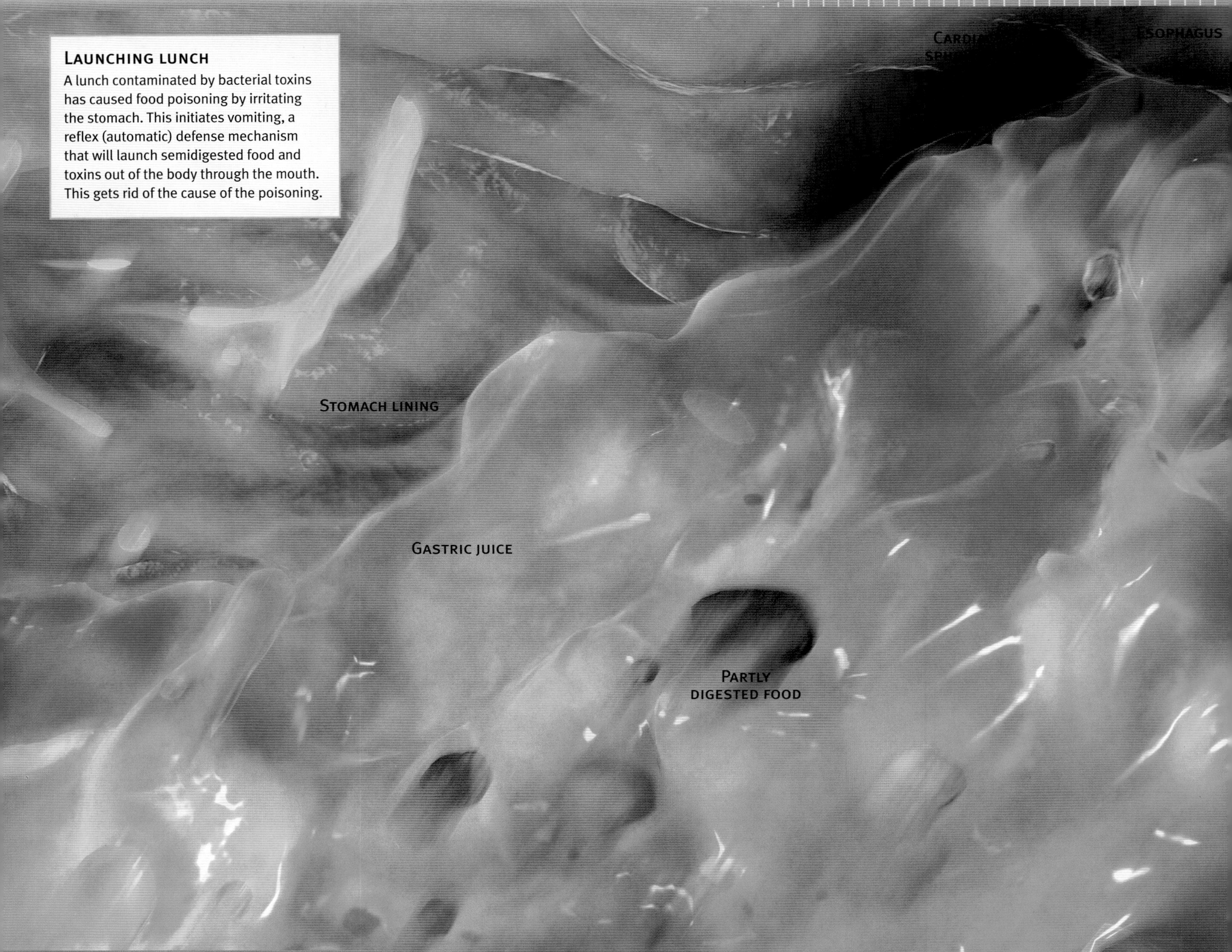

STOMACH LINING

GASTRIC JUICE

PARTLY DIGESTED FOOD

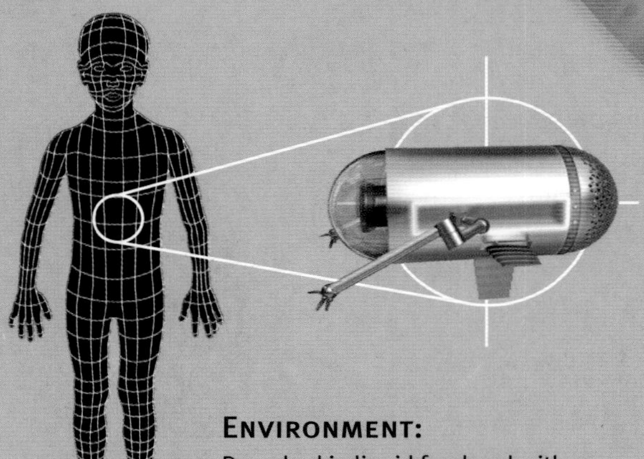

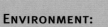

ENVIRONMENT:
Drenched in liquid food and with grappling hook ready, Nanocam rides the stomach contractions to record vomiting.

DIGESTION IN REVERSE

The muscular stomach, a J-shaped "bag" located under the ribs, plays two key roles in digestion. First, it partially digests food received through the esophagus. Second, the stomach stores semidigested food, releasing it slowly into the small intestines. But if the stomach lining is irritated, the process can be thrown into reverse, so vomiting occurs instead of digestion.

FIRST RESPONSES

- Irritation of the stomach lining detected by sensors and message is sent to brain.
- Skin sweats and mouth salivates, as nausea and stomach pain are experienced.
- Diaphragm and abdominal wall muscles contract—this compresses stomach and forces contents out of the mouth.

1 »

Stomach lining _____
Inner surface of the stomach wall, which houses glands that secrete gastric juice.

SENSITIVE STOMACH

A meal earlier in the day was contaminated with *Staphylococcus aureus* bacteria. These bacteria release a toxin into food that resists digestion and causes food poisoning. The toxin directly affects the stomach lining, causing irritation and pain, and making it appear red and inflamed.

2 »

Stomach contents _____
Partially digested food mixed with highly acidic gastric juice.

EARLY SIGNS OF ERUPTION

Sensors in the stomach lining send messages to the brain, which sets the vomiting reflex in motion. The diaphragm and abdominal wall muscles squeeze the stomach. In the pit of the stomach, the semidigested food—a mixture of soupy liquid and small, uncrushed chunks—starts to erupt.

3 »

Cardiac sphincter
Stops food being digested in the stomach from flowing back into the esophagus.

EMERGENCY EXIT

Guarding the entrance to the stomach from the esophagus is the cardiac sphincter. This is normally closed and only opens to allow recently swallowed food inside the stomach. But as pressure on the stomach mounts up, and its soupy contents get more compressed, the cardiac sphincter opens to let the vomit through.

4 »

Esophagus
Muscular tube that carries food from throat to stomach.

FINAL RELEASE

By now the feelings of discomfort and nausea are strong. In the buildup to being sick, heaving (dry retching) mimics the movements of vomiting, but without expelling any food. When pressure on the stomach peaks, food is forced up the esophagus, into the throat, and vomited out of the mouth.

DATA SEARCH

- The housefly (*Musca domestica*) regularly vomits up partially digested food—which can include human feces and dead animals—and eats it again. Something to think about when it lands on your lunch!

- Motion sickness, such as carsickness or seasickness, occurs when fluid in the inner ear is disturbed by movement. Balance sensors become confused and nausea is the result.

- Other causes of vomiting include excessive eating, so the stomach is overstretched, and irritation of the stomach lining by spicy foods or viruses.

- Gastric juice secreted by the stomach lining makes vomit acidic enough to strip paint or etch marble.

BRAIN

EYE MUSCLES

EYELID

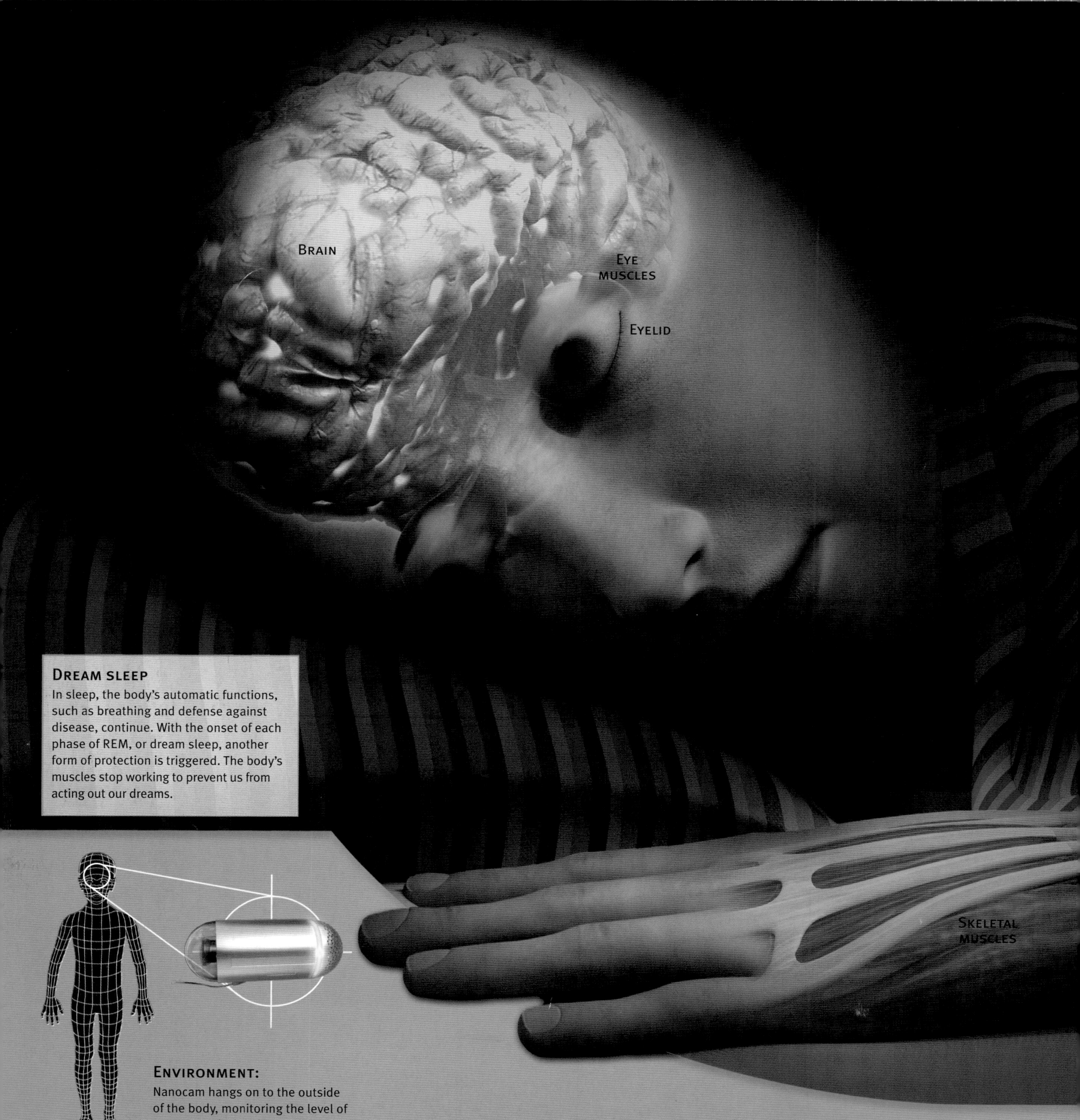

DREAM SLEEP

In sleep, the body's automatic functions, such as breathing and defense against disease, continue. With the onset of each phase of REM, or dream sleep, another form of protection is triggered. The body's muscles stop working to prevent us from acting out our dreams.

SKELETAL MUSCLES

ENVIRONMENT:

Nanocam hangs on to the outside of the body, monitoring the level of movement during dream sleep.

BRAIN ON AUTOMATIC

Every day the body goes through alternating cycles of sleep and wakefulness. Having spent two-thirds of the day awake and aware of its surroundings, the conscious brain switches off. However, other parts of the brain still automatically control vital functions such as heart rate. Sleep is essential to allow the body to rest and the brain to sort, collate, and store the day's experiences.

FIRST RESPONSES

- 24-hour body clock in the hypothalamus of the brain signals that it is time for sleep to begin.

- Brain stem slows activity of the cerebral hemispheres— the conscious brain.

- Sleep alternates between phases of deep sleep and longer phases of lighter, dream sleep.

1 »

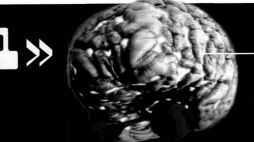

Brain
Controls body activities and enables us to think, feel, remember, and move.

2 »

Eyelid
Flap of skin that protects the eye and cleans it by blinking.

BUSY BRAIN

Sleep is underway and the first phase is deep sleep, when brain activity decreases and body functions slow down. This gives way to a phase of lighter dream sleep. Comparing the electrical brain waves generated shows that the brain is almost as active in dream sleep as it is when awake.

EYES UNDER COVER

During sleep the eyes are covered by the eyelids to stop them from drying out. Just behind the eyes, with the switch to REM sleep, the increasingly active brain consumes much more oxygen. At the same time, it orders an increase in heart rate, breathing rate, and body temperature.

3 »

Eye muscles
Six muscles anchored to the eye socket that pull on the eyeball to move it.

4 »

Skeletal muscles
Pull bones of the skeleton to move the body.

RAPID MOVEMENTS

REM stands for "rapid eye movement" and this is exactly what is happening under the closed eyelids. Most dreaming takes place during REM sleep. Some scientists believe the eye muscles pull the eyes upward, downward, and to the sides to follow the visual images that occur during dreams.

PROTECTED BY PARALYSIS

While the eye muscles keep busy, other skeletal muscles go limp during REM sleep. This temporary paralysis stops us acting out our dreams. Dreaming occurs as the brain carries out "housekeeping" duties, arranging the day's experiences and saving some in the memory. After REM sleep, the next phase of NREM (nonrapid eye movement) deep sleep begins.

DATA SEARCH

- The amount of sleep we require decreases as we get older. Infants need about 16 hours per day, school-aged children require 10 hours, young adults average 7 hours, and the elderly need 6 hours or less.

- Sleep is essential for general good health. People who are deprived of sleep for any length of time often experience extreme tiredness, headaches, confusion, and even hallucinations.

- Before the electric light bulb was invented in the 19th century, adults slept on average 10 hours every night.

- Disturbed by crying, new parents lose between 400 and 750 hours of sleep in the first year of their baby's life.

- The koala, an Australian marsupial mammal, lives on nutritionally poor eucalyptus leaves but saves energy by sleeping for 22 hours out of 24.

CONTINUING THE BATTLE

The body's defense force has an arsenal of chemicals ready to unleash on invading disease-causing pathogens. However, in some cases, they do not work.

Certain pathogens can evade the immune system and some bacteria release very fast-acting toxins. In these situations, help is needed to fight the invaders. Antibiotic drugs target and kill certain highly pathogenic bacteria. Vaccination kick-starts the immune response so it is prepared to launch an onslaught of pathogen-killing antibodies. More and more bacteria are becoming resistant to antibiotics, so for future combat, new solutions need to be found.

A SINGLE BACTERIUM DIVIDING EVERY 20 MINUTES HAS FIVE BILLION TRILLION OFFSPRING WITHIN 24 HOURS.

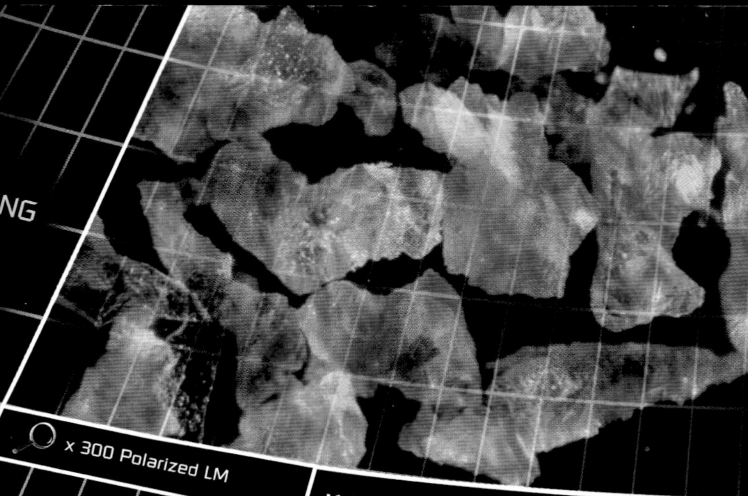

x 300 Polarized LM

x 140 Polarized LM

IN THE FUTURE, ANTIBIOTIC-RESISTANT BACTERIA MAY BE KILLED BY SPECIAL BACTERIOPHAGES—VIRUSES THAT INVADE BACTERIA.

INTERFERON

These are crystals of interferon, an antiviral protein produced naturally by cells that are infected with viruses. For example, when cold viruses invade nasal cells, these cells make and release interferon, which binds to nearby cells. If viruses try to invade these neighboring cells, interferon stops them from reproducing so the infection ends. Synthetic interferon is used to treat certain viral diseases.

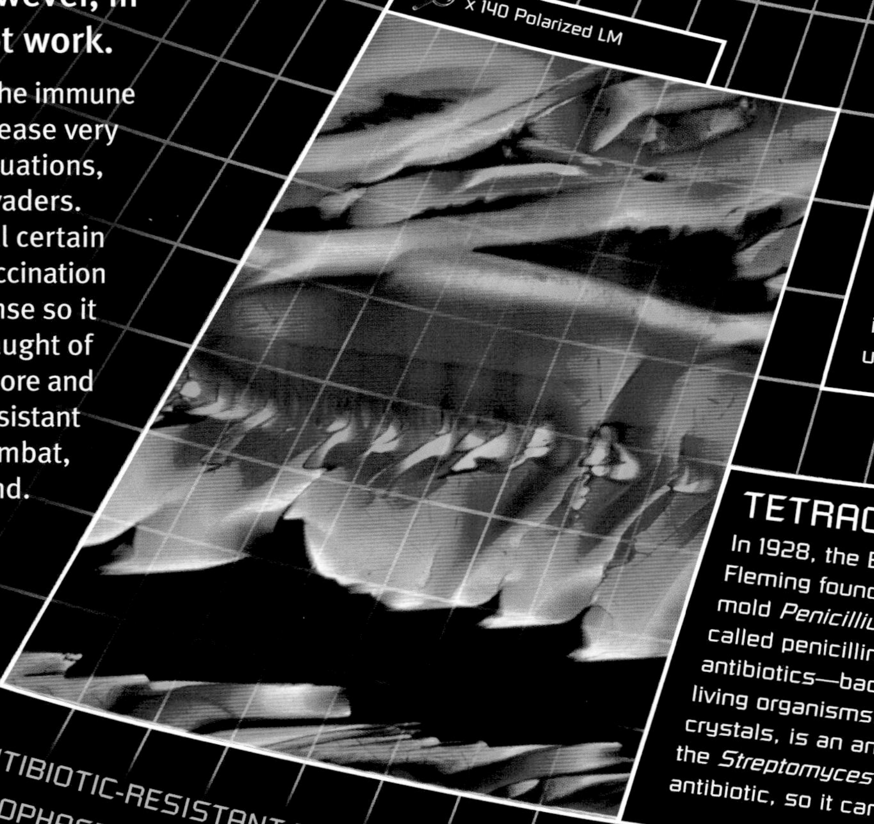

TETRACYCLINE

In 1928, the British researcher Alexander Fleming found that an extract from the fungal mold *Penicillium* killed bacteria. The extract, called penicillin, was to be the first of many antibiotics—bacteria-killing drugs derived from living organisms. Tetracycline, shown here as crystals, is an antibiotic derived from bacteria of the *Streptomyces* group. It is a broad-spectrum antibiotic, so it can kill many different bacteria.

KILLING BACTERIA

Antibiotics work by killing bacteria without harming body cells. They target processes at work inside bacterial cells but not present inside human cells. For example, many antibiotics disrupt the "machinery" that produces the tough, protective cell walls that surround bacteria. Human cells do not have such walls. With weakened cell walls, bacteria undergo lysis—or burst—as shown here. These *Staphylococcus aureus* bacteria (red) have burst, leaving only fragments (yellow) behind. *Staphylococcus aureus* causes a range of diseases from skin infections to blood poisoning.

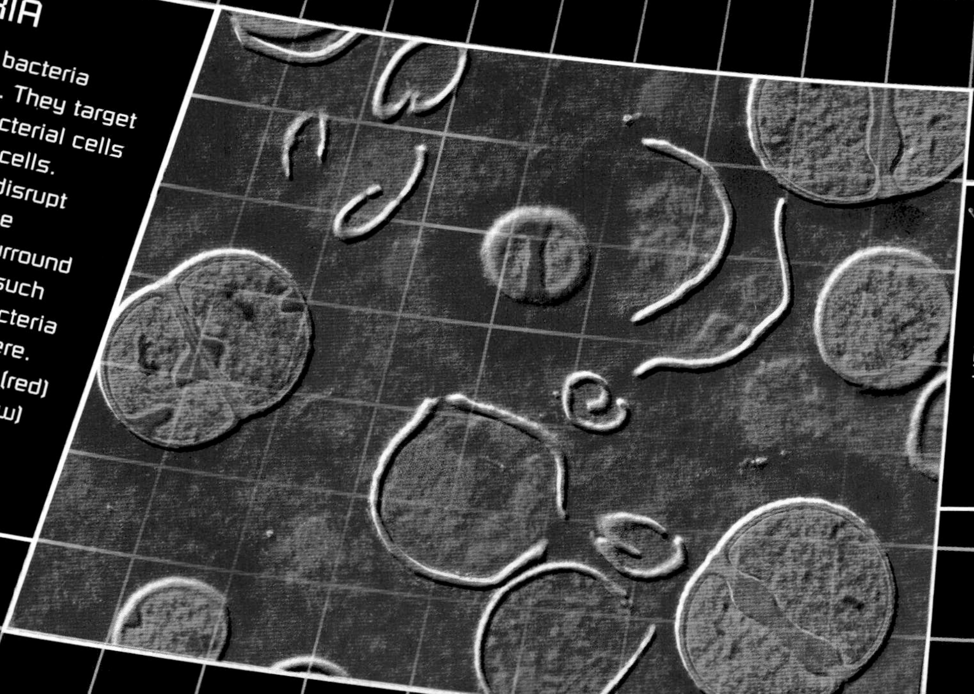

x 30,000 TEM

BEFORE ANTIBIOTIC DRUGS WERE AVAILABLE, BACTERIAL INFECTIONS FROM SIMPLE CUTS KILLED MANY PEOPLE EVERY YEAR.

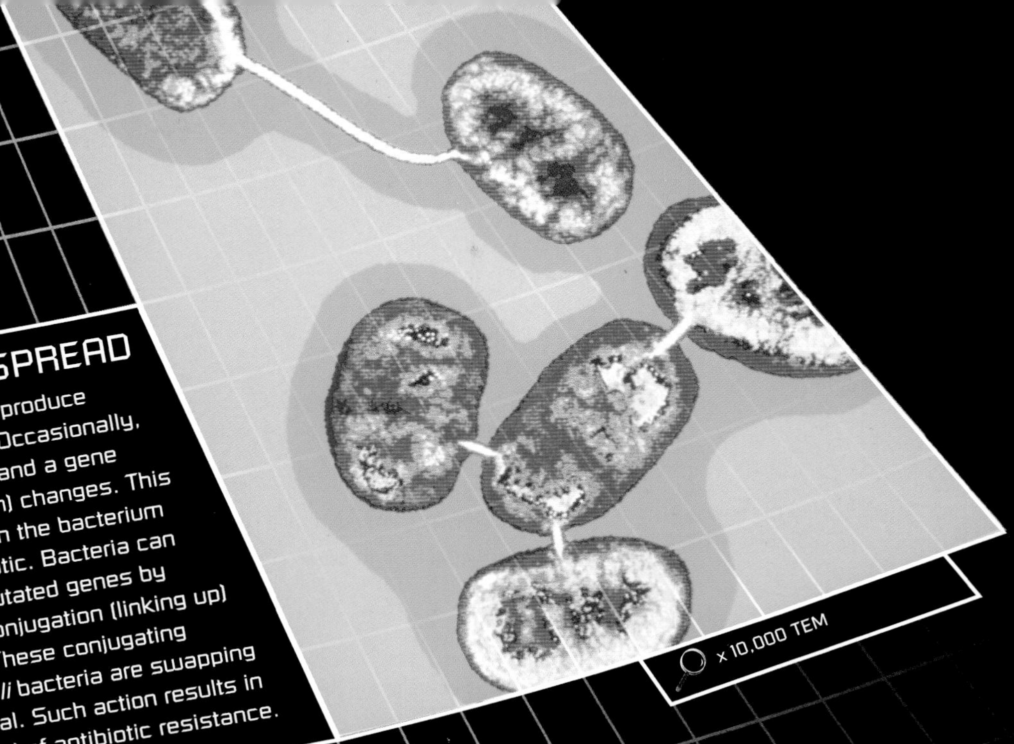

BACTERIAL SPREAD

Bacteria normally reproduce by splitting in two. Occasionally, a mutation occurs and a gene (genetic instruction) changes. This change may mean the bacterium resists an antibiotic. Bacteria can then pass on mutated genes by dividing or by conjugation (linking up) as seen here. These conjugating *Escherichia coli* bacteria are swapping genetic material. Such action results in the fast spread of antibiotic resistance.

x 10,000 TEM

x 30,000 TEM

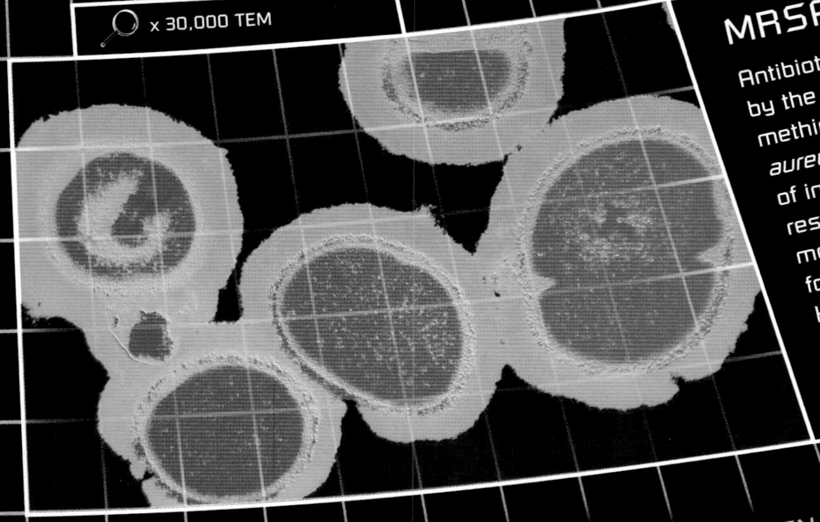

MRSA

Antibiotic resistance is being fueled by the overuse of antibiotics. These methicillin-resistant *Staphylococcus aureus* (MRSA) bacteria are an example of increasingly common antibiotic resistance. They remain unaffected by most antibiotics. The bacterium is often found in the skin and nose of healthy people. However, in hospitals it causes major problems by infecting the wounds of sick patients who already have low immunity.

VACCINATIONS PROTECT CHILDREN AGAINST VIRAL DISEASES, SUCH AS MEASLES AND MUMPS, AND BACTERIAL DISEASES, SUCH AS DIPHTHERIA AND TETANUS.

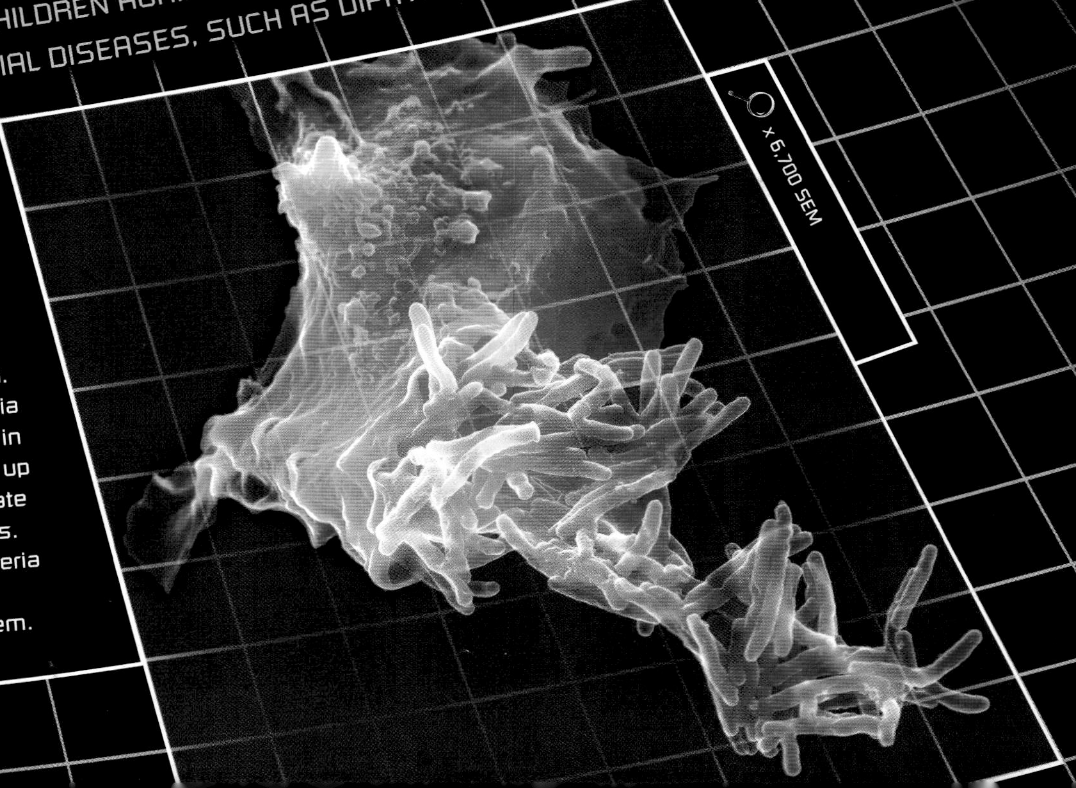

x 6,700 SEM

VACCINATIONS

First used at the end of the 18th century, vaccination trains the immune system to recognize and fight a pathogen that would otherwise overcome it. Most vaccines are made from a specific germ, but weakened so it does not cause harm. Here, weakened TB (tuberculosis) bacteria (blue) have been injected into the body in the form of a vaccine. They are rounded up by a macrophage (red) that will stimulate white blood cells to produce antibodies. In future, if any real pathogenic TB bacteria invade, there will be no delay before antibodies are released to destroy them.

GLOSSARY

A

ABDOMEN (HUMAN)
Lower part of the trunk (the central part of the body), between the chest and the hips, which contains most of the digestive organs.

ABDOMEN (INSECT)
Rearmost of the three sections of an insect's body. The others are the head and thorax.

ACIDIC
Describes a liquid that has the properties of an acid that can, for example, dissolve the surface of teeth or form gastric juice.

ADRENAL GLAND
One of two glands, each located on top of a kidney, which release the hormone adrenalin.

ALKALINE
Describes a liquid, such as saliva, which can neutralize (make neutral) acids.

ALLERGEN
Normally harmless substance, such as pollen, which triggers an allergy—the overreaction of the body's immune system.

ANTIBIOTIC
Drug derived from a living organism that kills pathogenic bacteria.

ANTIBODY
Substance released by lymphocytes of the immune system that targets a specific pathogen and marks it for destruction.

ANTICOAGULANT
Substance that prevents the formation of blood clots, secreted by blood-feeding parasites such as head lice.

ANTIGEN
"Foreign" substance that triggers the immune system to defend the body.

ANTIVIRAL
Describes a drug that kills viruses.

ARTERY
Blood vessel that carries oxygen-rich blood from the heart to the tissues.

ARTHRITIS
General term that describes diseases that affect the joints of the skeleton and limit movement.

ATRIUM (PLURAL ATRIA)
One of two (left and right) upper chambers of the heart.

AXON
Also called a nerve fiber, the long "tail" of a neuron that transmits nerve impulses to another neuron or muscle fiber.

B

BACTERIA (SINGULAR: BACTERIUM)
Group of simple, single-celled microorganisms. Some of them can cause disease in humans.

BICEPS BRACHII
Muscle that bends the arm at the elbow.

BRAIN STEM
Part of the brain that controls basic life processes such as breathing and heart rate.

BRONCHI (SINGULAR BRONCHUS)
Branches of the trachea (windpipe) that divide into further bronchi inside the lungs.

BRONCHIOLE
Branch of a bronchus, and smallest airway in the lung.

C

CALCIUM
Mineral that forms the hard part of bones and teeth.

CAPILLARY
Tiny blood vessel that carries blood between arteries and veins.

CELL
Microscopic living unit, trillions of which make up the human body.

CEREBRAL HEMISPHERES
Two halves of the cerebrum—the largest part of the brain, which is involved in conscious thought.

CERUMEN
Waxy secretion produced by lining of ear canal.

CILIA
Microscopic, hairlike structures that project from the surface of certain cells.

CILIATED CELL
Cell that carries cilia on its surface.

COLLAGEN
Tough, fibrous protein that strengthens connective tissues such as bone and cartilage.

CORTICOSTEROID
Steroid hormone released by the adrenal gland that is involved in the immune response, and a synthetic drug that is used to reduce inflammation.

CT (COMPUTED TOMOGRAPHY) SCAN
Technique that uses X-rays and a computer to produce images of living tissues.

D

DISEASE
Disorder caused by a malfunction in one or more body systems.

DNA (DEOXYRIBONUCLEIC ACID)
One of a number of large molecules found inside a cell that carry the instructions for its construction and operation.

E

EPIDERMIS
Upper protective layer of the skin from which dead cells are lost constantly as skin flakes.

EPIGLOTTIS

Flap of cartilage that folds over, sealing the entrance to the larynx during swallowing.

G

GASTRIC

Describes something relating to the stomach.

GENE

One of the "instructions" carried on genetic material, such as DNA.

GENETIC MATERIAL

General name for molecules such as DNA that carry the instructions to build an organism.

GERM

General term for a microorganism, especially a bacterium, which causes disease.

GLAND

Tissue or organ that produces a substance, such as adrenalin or sweat, which is released into or onto the body.

GLUCOSE

Body's primary energy source, and main sugar circulating in the blood.

GLYCOGEN

Large carbohydrate molecule made up of glucose units that is the main energy store in the liver and muscles.

GOBLET CELL

Type of epithelial cell that produces mucus.

H

HAIR FOLLICLE

Deep pit in the skin from which a hair grows.

HISTAMINE

Substance released by cells that triggers inflammation.

TYPES OF BODY CELLS

The human body is constructed from about 100 trillion microscopic, living building blocks called cells. There are more than 200 types of cells that vary in shape, size, location, and the job they do. However, they all share the same basic structure.

RODS AND CONES

Found in the eye and named for their cell shape, rods (yellow) and cones (blue) are photoreceptors. They detect light and send nerve impulses to the brain, enabling us to see.

x 750 SEM

KIDNEY CELL

Located inside each kidney, this tubular cell is covered in folds. These greatly increase its surface area for absorbing water back into the bloodstream, in order to concentrate urine.

x 5,200 SEM

FAT CELL

This section through a fat cell shows most of the space inside taken up by oil droplets (yellow) that push the nucleus (purple) to one side. Fat cells store energy and insulate the body.

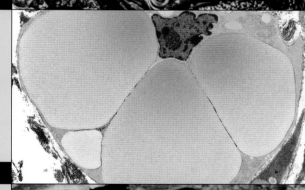

x 1,000 TEM

BONE CELL

An osteocyte, or bone cell, sits isolated inside its lacuna (space) surrounded by hard bone tissue. Bone cells are responsible for maintaining all the body's bones.

x 5,000 SEM

GLIAL CELLS

These star-shaped astrocytes (green) support neurons, the cells that carry nerve impulses. Astrocytes belong to the glial cells that make up 90 percent of nervous system cells.

x 165 LM

GLOSSARY

HORMONE
Chemical messenger released into the blood by endocrine (hormonal) glands such as the adrenal gland, which alters the activities of target tissues.

HYPOTHALAMUS
Small, multitasking part of the brain that controls many body activities including sweating.

I

IMMUNE SYSTEM
Collective defense measures, including phagocytes and antibodies, which protect the body from invading, disease-causing organisms.

INFLAMMATION
Redness, swelling, heat, and pain produced by the body as a defensive reaction to injury or infection.

INSECT
A member of a large group of animals without a backbone that have six legs, wings, and a body divided into three parts. Bees belong to this group.

INSOLUBLE
Describes a substance that does not dissolve in water.

K

KERATIN
Tough, waterproof substance found in flattened, dead cells in the skin's upper epidermis.

KERATINOCYTE
Main type of cell in the skin's epidermis.

KIDNEY
One of two bean-shaped organs located in the back of the abdomen that produce urine.

L

LARYNX
Also known as the voice box, this organ is situated between the throat and trachea and contains the vocal cords and produces sounds.

LM (LIGHT MICROGRAPH)
Photograph of a magnified specimen produced using a light microscope.

LYMPHOCYTE
White blood cell that plays a key role in the immune system by releasing antibodies.

M

MACROPHAGE
Type of white blood cell that targets and consumes pathogens.

MAST CELL
Type of cell found in the tissues that stores and releases histamine and plays a key role in inflammation and allergies.

MELANIN
Brown-black pigment (coloring) found in the skin and hair.

MELANOCYTE
Cell in the epidermis that produces melanin.

MICROORGANISM
Organism that is so small it can only be seen with a microscope, such as a bacterium.

MOTOR NEURON
Nerve cell that transmits nerve impulses from the brain or spinal cord to muscles and glands.

KEY BODY TISSUES
Body cells of the same type are grouped together in a tissue that performs a specific task. Although there are many tissue varieties, all belong to four key categories—epithelial, connective, nervous, and muscular tissues. These tissues cover, support, control, and move the body.

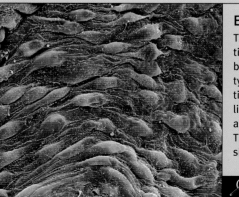
 x 860 SEM

EPITHELIAL TISSUE
This is an epithelial tissue that lines the blood vessels. Other types of epithelial tissue, or epithelium, line the respiratory and digestive systems. They also form the skin's upper layer.

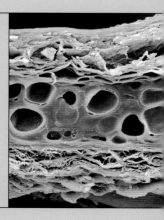

MUCUS
Thick, protective fluid secreted by the lining of the respiratory and digestive systems.

MUSCLE
Organ that uses energy to contract (get shorter) in order to move the body.

MUTATION
Change in the genetic material of an organism.

N

NASAL CAVITY
Hollow space behind the nose through which air flows during breathing.

NECTAR
Sugary liquid produced by flowers to attract pollinating insects such as bees.

NERVE
Cablelike bundle of the axons of neurons that relay nerve impulses between the body and the spinal cord and brain.

NERVE FIBER
See axon.

NERVE IMPULSE
Tiny electrical signal that travels along a neuron at high speed.

NEURON
One of the billions of nerve cells that form the nervous system and carry nerve impulses.

NEUTRALIZE
Adding one liquid to another so that the latter is neither acidic nor alkaline.

NEUTROPHIL
Type of white blood cell that targets and consumes pathogens.

NUCLEUS
Control center of a cell, which contains its genetic material.

O

ORGAN
Body part, such as the heart or brain, that is made up of two or more tissues and which has a specific role.

OXYGEN
Gas found in the air, taken into the body during breathing, and used by cells to release energy from glucose.

P

PAPILLAE (SINGULAR: PAPILLA)
Small bumps projecting from the tongue's surface, some of which house taste buds.

PARASITE
Organism that lives on or in, and benefits from, another organism.

PATHOGEN
Microorganism such as a bacterium or virus that causes disease.

PHAGOCYTES
White blood cells such as neutrophils and macrophages that eat and destroy pathogens.

PHEROMONE
Chemical released into the air by one animal that has an effect on another, such as the alarm pheromone released by bees.

PLATELET
Cell fragment carried by the blood that plays a key role in clotting.

POLLEN
Tiny particles released by flowers that contain male reproductive cells.

PORE
Tiny opening such as a sweat pore in the skin.

PROTEIN
One of a group of substances that perform many roles in the body. Other examples are enzymes and antibodies.

PUBERTY
Period during the early teenage years when the body grows rapidly and changes into adult form.

PUS
Whitish fluid that contains dead phagocytes engorged with pathogens.

CONNECTIVE TISSUE
Sandwiched between skin layers (pink), elastic cartilage (green) shapes and supports the ear flap. Other types of connective tissues include bone, tendon, and adipose (fat) tissue.

○ x 25 SEM

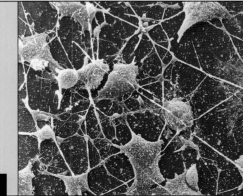

NERVOUS TISSUE
Found only in the nervous system, nervous tissue contains impulse-carrying neurons and support cells. These interlinked neurons in the brain form a complex control network.

○ x 1,860 SEM

MUSCULAR TISSUE
This type of tissue performs many tasks, including moving limbs, pushing food along the intestines, and pumping blood. This view shows the inside of a fiber (cell) of cardiac muscle tissue in the heart.

○ x 5,000 SEM

GLOSSARY

R

RECEPTOR
Nerve cell that responds to a stimulus, such as light or touch, by triggering a nerve impulse that passes along a sensory neuron.

REFLEX
Split-second, automatic, unconscious response to a stimulus that commonly protects the body from danger.

RELAY NEURON
Nerve cell found in the brain and spinal cord that transmits nerve impulses from one neuron to another, and also processes information.

RIBS
Twelve pairs of bones that curve forward from the backbone to form a protective cage around the heart and lungs.

S

SCALD
Burn caused by steam or hot water.

SEM (SCANNING ELECTRON MICROGRAPH)
Photograph of a magnified specimen produced using a scanning electron microscope.

SENSORY NEURON
Nerve cell that transmits nerve impulses to the brain or spinal cord from receptors.

SINOATRIAL NODE
Small region of modified muscle in the heart that triggers heartbeats, thereby acting as a pacemaker.

SKELETAL MUSCLES
Muscles that pull bones to move the body.

SOLUBLE
Describes a substance that dissolves in water.

SPECIES
A group of living things such as humans that can breed together.

SPHINCTER
Ring of muscle around a passage or opening that opens or closes to control the flow of material along or through it.

SYMPATHETIC NERVOUS SYSTEM
Part of the nervous system that automatically activates a wide range of organs, and helps the body deal with stress.

SYNAPSE
Junction between two neurons or between a neuron and a muscle fiber.

SYSTEM
A group of linked organs, such as the digestive system, that work together to carry out a specific function or functions.

T

TB (TUBERCULOSIS)
Bacterial disease that affects the lungs and sometimes other organs.

TEM (TRANSMISSION ELECTRON MICROGRAPH)
Photograph of a magnified specimen produced using a transmission electron microscope.

TISSUE
Group of cells of the same or similar type that carry out a specific function.

TOOTH DECAY
Disease in which acids released by bacteria keep eating away at the enamel of a tooth and expose its interior.

TOXIN
Poisonous substance released by a pathogenic bacterium.

TRACHEA
Also known as windpipe, the tube that links the larynx to the bronchi and carries air toward and away from the lungs.

U

UREA
Waste substance produced by the liver that is removed from the body in urine by the kidneys.

URETHRA
Tube that carries urine from the bladder and out of the body.

V

VEIN
Blood vessel that carries oxygen-poor blood from the tissues to the heart.

VENOM
Poisonous liquid produced by one animal and injected into another animal by a sting or a bite.

VENTRICLE
One of two (left and right) lower chambers of the heart.

VERTEBRAE (SINGULAR: VERTEBRA)
One of the chain of irregularly shaped bones that makes up the backbone, spine, or vertebral column.

VIRUS
Tiny, infectious nonliving agent that causes disease by invading, and multiplying inside, body cells.

W

WATER VAPOR
Gas found in the air produced when water evaporates.

WHITE BLOOD CELL
Type of cell found in the blood that is involved in defending the body against pathogens.

WITHDRAWAL REFLEX
Automatic action that pulls a body part away from danger.

BODY SYSTEMS

The human body is organized in different levels, with similar cells grouped into tissues. Two or more types of tissue form an organ. Organs that work together form a system. The body has 12 systems in total and some of them are shown here.

The other four systems that make up the body are the lymphatic system, the male and female reproductive systems, and the integumentary system (consisting of skin, hair, and nails).

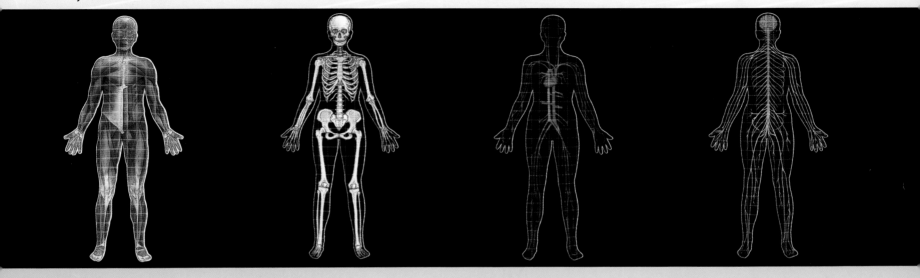

MUSCULAR SYSTEM
More than 640 skeletal muscles are attached to the bones of the skeleton by tough tendons. They contract (get shorter), pulling bones across flexible joints to move the body.

SKELETAL SYSTEM
This strong but flexible framework of 206 bones, cartilage, and ligaments surrounds and protects the soft internal organs, shapes the body, and allows it to move.

CIRCULATORY SYSTEM
Consisting of the heart, a network of blood vessels, and blood, this system supplies essentials to body cells, removes waste from body cells, and helps the body to fight infection.

NERVOUS SYSTEM
The body's main control system has the brain and spinal cord at its core. Through nerves that reach all body parts, the brain and spinal cord process received information and send out instructions.

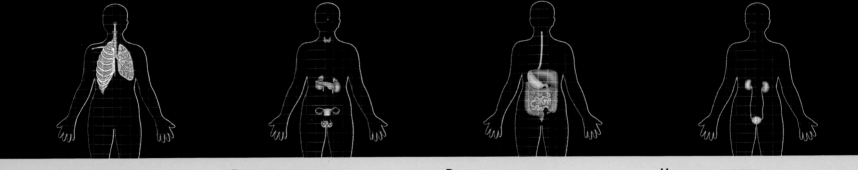

RESPIRATORY SYSTEM
Breathing moves air in and out of the airways and lungs. These are the major components of the respiratory system. Oxygen from the air is used by cells to release life-giving energy.

ENDOCRINE SYSTEM
This system consists of a number of glands that release chemical messengers, called hormones, into the blood. These control many processes including growth and reproduction.

DIGESTIVE SYSTEM
Made up of the mouth, esophagus, stomach, intestines, and linked organs, such as the liver and pancreas, this system takes in and processes food so it can be used by the body.

URINARY SYSTEM
The two kidneys process blood in order to make waste urine. This liquid is transported by the ureters to the bladder where it is stored before being passed along the urethra and out of the body.

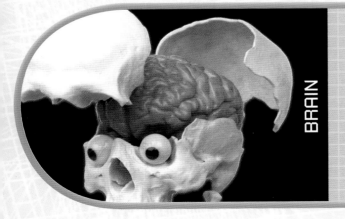

BRAIN

The most complex organ on the planet is the human brain. It makes up just 2 percent of the body's weight, yet consumes 20 percent of its energy. A high-speed communication network made up of 100 billion interconnected neurons makes all aspects of consciousness possible, such as thought, memory, imagination, learning, movement, and vision. At the same time, the brain automatically and unconsciously regulates our breathing and heart rates.

INDEX

CREDITS

Richard Walker would like to thank all those who have contributed to producing this book. Particular thanks go to Andrea Mills, Joanne Little, Samantha Richiardi, Julie Ferris, and other members of the DK team for their enthusiasm and diligence, to NIKID for their creativity, and to consultant Dr. Sue Davidson for her invaluable scrutiny of the images and text.

DK would like to thank:
NIKID DESIGN LTD www.nikid.co.uk
Principle 2d Designer Lee Allan Principle 3d Designer Jason Harding

The publisher would like to thank the following for their kind permission to reproduce their photographs: (Key: a-above; b-below/bottom; c-center; l-left; r-right; t-top)
Dennis Kunkel Microscopy, Inc.: 28tc, 64c. Science Photo Library: 15bl, 15cr, 65br; Dr. Jeremy Burgess 37bl; CNRI 67cra; A. B. Dowsett 40br; Eye Of Science 28bl, 29br, 40c, 41cl; P. Ferguson, Ism 64bc; Phillip A. Harrington, Peter Arnold Inc. 64tr; Nancy Kedersha 67br; Dr. Kari Lounatmaa 65cl; Prof. P. Motta/Dept. Of Anatomy/ University "La Sapienza," Rome 67crb; Professors P. Motta & F. Carpino/ Univer- Sity "La Sapienza," Rome 52bl; Professors P. Motta & T. Naguro 11bl; Professors P.M. Motta & F.M. Magliocca 41tc; Susumu Nishinaga 14c, 52tc, 53br; Omikron 67tr; Alfred Pasieka 40tr, 47bl; Photo Insolite Realite 29tc; Jean-Claude Revy, ISM 33bl; Steve Gschmeissner 14cb, 19bl, 25bl, 52cr, 53tc, 67cr, 70bc, 70br, 71bl, 71br; Dave Roberts 15tl; Dr. Linda Stannard, Uct 65tc; Andrew Syred 14tr, 28cr, 29cl, 41br, 53cl.

All other images © Dorling Kindersley
For further information see:
www.dkimages.com